Auto Free Design

Dan Paul

Eric Hiltner

Copyright © 2024 by Dan Paul

All rights reserved.

No part of this book may be reproduced in any form or by any electronic or mechanical means, including information storage and retrieval systems, without written permission from the author, except for the use of brief quotations in a book review.

❋ Created with Vellum

Contents

Transition to Sustain our Future	v
1. Functions of a Progressive Transport System	1
2. 10 Points on Sustainable Transportation	12
3. AFD Safety	21
4. AFD Why	36
5. AFD Philosophy of Design	48
6. AFD Examples	64
7. AFD Global Warming Solutions for Transport	79
8. Auto Free Cities	86
9. Benefits of AFD	101
10. AFD How to Get Rid of Your Car	117
About the Author	129
Also by Dan Paul	131

Transition to Sustain our Future

After 250 years of fossil fuel use, humans have produced the conditions for human extinction. In these conditions, buildings and vehicles that require oil, gas, or other fossil fuels generate emissions that cause climate change. Climate change increases the frequency, intensity, and duration of extreme weather. Climate change destabilizes weather patterns required to grow crops, maintain buildings, and for people to live.

Transport Solutions to Reduce Global Warming

Auto Free Design integrates transport solutions that reduce emissions that cause global warming. Humans adapt as conditions make it impossible to continue to use fossil fuels. Through change of mind and action, people generate solutions.

My five-year-old brother was run over by a driver who could barely see the road. I've driven a car over creeks and into trees and had to fix them on the side of the road. After ten years of using cars, trucks, and motorcycles, I've learned to live without a vehicle and travel coast to coast, country to country, and city to country without a vehicle. Yes, there are significant challenges to living without a car, and yes, it can be done without too much trouble. With a will, there's a way.

After saying goodbye to vehicles and living a richer, fuller life, the benefits are many, including the following:

- less stress

- less danger

- less fear of catastrophe

- less need for money

- more stable and predictable life

- massive improvement in your quality of life.

- freedom from oppressive conditions of auto use

- why move cars when you can move yourself

Of course, I had to pay a price. I ride a bicycle in the rain, snow, sleet, and sunshine. I've walked and used transit under the same conditions. Living without a vehicle isn't difficult; it's more pleasant and sustainable and helps me live the principles I believe in.

If you want to make the most significant improvement in your life, get rid of your vehicles and experience freedom from the automobile. It's here and now, ready for you to live beyond the shackles of owning, using, and fixing a vehicle. To go beyond the mediocre and embrace life for people, not cars. Imagine never thinking about getting into a car crash, dealing with bigot cops or drivers, and endless bills to pay. All for something that only loses value.

Chapter 1
Functions of a Progressive Transport System

Priorities of a Transport System

To make our country more sustainable, we can change our transportation system from one that is dependent on automobiles to one that prioritizes walking, bicycling, and using transit. As auto use is reduced and people begin to use sustainable modes of transport, we will gain many benefits. If we combine a rapid transit system with a transit-oriented design, we can create a way for people to walk, bicycle, or use transit to meet their needs.

Prioritize Non-Motorized Transport

As we build a safer, healthier, and sustainable city/region, we can change our transportation system from one that depends on automobiles to one that prioritizes non-motorized transport (walking, bicycling) and transit (buses, rail). Reducing auto use while increasing walking, bicycling, and using transit will encourage people to exercise more, reduce pollution, reduce the cost of living, and reduce dependence on scarce resources while improving the quality of life.

Reducing Pavement Generates Benefits

Fewer cars and less traffic can make our cities safer. If people switch from car use to walking, bicycling, and using transit, then more people will use safer ways to travel. If those people are walking and bicycling in areas that exclude automobiles, they will have no chance of an auto accident. As the infrastructure of the region begins to accommodate pedestrians and bicycle users, the region will reduce transportation costs. With fewer roadways to construct, maintain, and patrol, government outlays for transportation may be reduced.

Reducing Pollution Generates Solutions

Reducing air pollution from vehicles can make regions healthier places to live. Cleaner air can reduce health care costs, pain, suffering, and death for people with respiratory problems and provide better air for plants, animals, and people. Soot from diesel engines damages lungs, plants, and animals while deteriorating the exterior of buildings. Cities can reduce diesel soot pollution by putting pressure on the Federal government to require diesel engines to use clean technology. Particulate traps and fuel oxidizing technology reduce diesel soot. Governments must govern how much pollution vehicles exhaust to minimize pain and suffering in people, reduce healthcare costs, and reduce the destruction of plants, animals, and buildings.

Priorities of a transport system

- Move people and goods safely without generating pollution.
- Move people and goods using sustainable infrastructure.
- Move people and goods using sustainable methods.

Walking and Bicycling are Healthier Ways to Move than Auto Use

If these changes occur region-wide, significant reductions in healthcare expenditures may accrue. If people walk and bicycle more, healthcare savings will increase as people become healthier by exercising more. Reducing health care costs should be a priority for a transport system

Separating Traffic Modes

Governments can separate motorized and non-motorized transport. Fewer streets should reduce modal conflict between pedestrians, bicyclists, cars, buses, and trucks. Reducing interactions between pedestrians, bicycles, and vehicles may increase safety. Walkways over or under busy streets lessen the chances of an accident between vehicles and non-motorized transport. Expanding car-free areas can separate automobiles from places where people live and work.

What's the Problem?

If we admit that the transportation system is causing problems, we can begin to resolve those problems. If we don't realize there is a problem, there will be no reason to make changes. Making changes will result in benefits. If we admit the issues and make changes, we can receive the benefits.

I Want My Car

Not everything improves with Auto Free Design. Some people will lose, and some people will gain. People who insist on using automobiles when they can walk, ride bicycles, or use transit may not like an auto-free system. It may take some time for people to adapt.

As the economy changes, new jobs will open up for people who lose their careers in the auto industry. An auto-free transport system will generate jobs. Workers can change the infrastructure, construct and maintain other land uses, and run an expanded transit system.

Sustainable Methods Generate Benefits

To reduce health care costs, increase the quality of life, and make the city more pleasant, city regions can reduce auto use while increasing non-motorized transport. As the system locates development that meets needs within walking distance near transit stops, the city region will move closer to a sustainable system.

Eco-Footprint of Transport Methods

Walking, cycling, and using transit are more sustainable than auto use. Manufacturing, distributing, and disposing of automobiles require vast resources, energy, and people power. Without a costly, comprehensive, and environmentally damaging system of roads, automobiles will go nowhere. Compare this to another system. Imagine living in an area the size of several blocks with a few streets for service and emergency vehicles but not cars. Parking would be outside an auto-free zone, underground, or in vertical parking lots, and sometimes not at all. Less pavement for parking in a car-free area would not be needed, police patrols for auto users would not be required, less infrastructure would be needed, less healthcare would be necessary for the victims of an auto accident, and less industrial production would be generated. As a society, we could live better with less money, less work, and less danger from global warming.

Prevent Oil Wars With Sustainable Methods

A sustainable city requires limiting our use of resources so that the environment will support life into the future. Countries are fighting to control oil, a crucial element in the auto economy. The quest for adequate supplies of oil and profits is undermining a just, equitable, and democratic foreign policy. As oil resources dwindle, the fight to control the oil will intensify. But this drive to control the resources could be reduced if we pursue other ways of moving people and goods. An auto-free economy reduces oil use, conserves energy, and can use renewable energy sources.

Improving the Health of Humans and Transport

Reducing health care and transportation costs can be done in many regions with minimal effort. If the city sets up the conditions for people to walk, bicycle, and use transit to meet their needs, they will get more exercise, and this can reduce visits to clinics and hospitals. Cities must be set up so people can meet their needs a short distance away. Pressuring the city to provide sustainable transportation is in the interest of businesses that compete with other regions worldwide. Regions that reduce transport and healthcare costs will have a competitive edge over auto-oriented areas.

Goals of Auto-Free Design

Auto-free design is a process of moving from a transport system in which people must use an automobile to live to a transportation system that allows people to live without using a car. A better transportation system is one in which non-motorized transport and transit are the fastest, cheapest, and most sustainable way to move between two points. In many cities and rural areas worldwide, people must own a vehicle to go to work, school, shops, and clinics. One way to increase freedom is to create the means for people to live without owning an automobile.

High and Low-Density Development

Sprawl, or low-density development, requires large amounts of infrastructure per capita. Infrastructure includes roads, utilities, and public services. Public services include the police department, fire department, schools, libraries, and water. Often, sprawl doesn't include public services people take for granted in the city. Some city services are stretched to the limits to serve the suburbs as they must extend from the city to the suburbs. Spread-out development increases the response time of emergency vehicles since they have to travel farther and may have to sit in congested traffic. Transit-oriented development is designed to allow more people per infrastructure to use the transport infrastructure, utilities, and public services. As more people use the same infrastructure, the price per person decreases as service delivery becomes more efficient.

Suburbs Drain Money from the City

When the city spends money to provide infrastructure for low-density development near the city's limits, resources are drained from infrastructure projects within the city. Schools, libraries, police, and fire departments may lose money when the city spends on roads, sewers, and water lines for sprawling developments around freeway exits. As land outside the city is developed, farmland, green space, and rural countryside disappear as highway projects expand auto-oriented development. Since poor people can't own vehicles, the suburbs are for wealthier people. In some cities, sprawl serves white populations as it drains money for infrastructure projects for minorities in the city.

Low and High Density

Sprawl and transit-oriented development are opposites. Sprawl is compatible with an auto-oriented transportation system, while transit-oriented development is compatible with non-motorized transport (walking, bicycling) and transit infrastructure (bus, rail). Sprawl is a low-density development, and transit-oriented design is a high-density development. Living in the suburbs requires auto use, while the transit-oriented design does not require auto use.

Regions Shift to Non-Motorized Transport

Auto-free design creates the means for people to live without a car. Fortunately for some, this is the case in many places, but many people must use a vehicle to live. As regions shift from auto use to non-motorized transport and transit, more people can live without automobiles. As cities increase infrastructure for walking, bicycling, and rapid transit, the benefits accrue for many people.

Benefits of AFD

For people to live without an automobile, the means to meet needs should be located near housing. If many people live in a small area, there will be enough people to keep shops and clinics open. To do this requires high densities of people and mixed-use development. Mixed-use development allows different kinds of land uses to occupy the same area. This provides a way to live a short walk to the grocery store, restaurant, clothing store, or clinic. Many cities do not allow this now or were set up when mixed-use zoning wasn't common or desirable. In those cities, single-use zoning is more common. Single-use zoning does not allow residential housing to mix with office space, restaurants, or clinics. In these areas, the distances between shops and housing are so large that people must use a car to travel.

Sustainable Transport and Development

Auto-free design combines sustainable transport with sustainable development. Walking and bicycling are sustainable transportation. Sustainable development orients meeting needs within walking distance or transit stops. Meeting needs include what people need to live. Schools, parks, jobs, restaurants, and clothing stores can be located so that people can walk, bicycle, or use transit to get there. Transit use is more sustainable than auto use. Transit-oriented development is more sustainable than sprawl. Auto-free development, which allows people to meet their needs without a car, is more sustainable than transit-oriented development. Combining transit and development can make safe, pleasant, and sustainable places for people to live.

Transition to Sustainable

Auto-free design is a progressive direction for transportation and development that offers advantages to lead to a brighter future. Sustainable transport, which includes walking, cycling, and using transit, is safer, healthier, and more sustainable than car use. In the bigger picture, sustainable transportation leads to a more stable, secure, and viable environment, economic system, and foreign policy. Right now, auto use is killing and injuring many people and pushing us into difficult and dangerous environmental, economic, and foreign policy circumstances. We can begin a brighter future by making small changes now.

Towards an Auto-Free City

What changes move us toward an auto-free city? Three actions will move us toward a better future. Reducing auto use, increasing sustainable transport, and transit-oriented development will set the conditions for sustainable transport and development. Governments that care about the future of their city, region, and nation take measures to reduce auto use. Increasing the costs of using an automobile by increasing the gas tax, charging tolls in congested areas, and improving sustainable transport infrastructure are ways to reduce auto use. Providing better walkways and bike lanes integrated into a regional rapid transit system can create the conditions for people to live without automobiles. As appropriate development is situated around transit stops, people can meet their needs without leaving their neighborhood.

Towards Freedom from the Automobile

Auto-free design moves from an auto-oriented transportation and development system to a transportation and development system that allows people to walk to meet their needs. It avoids coercive measures in favor of positive solutions. If a transit infrastructure is set up to enable people to travel cheaper, faster, and more efficiently by walking, bicycling, and using transit than automobiles, even car users will choose transit. Cities that want to create a brighter future for their citizens can integrate auto-free design into their long-term plans. The cities, corporations, and nonprofits that are the first to incorporate these designs will have an edge over others as auto-free cities reduce transport and healthcare expenses per capita. The first ones to develop the auto-free direction can export those ideas and actions to other locations.

Consensus Movement to Freedom from Auto Use

A gradual process can transform a region from auto-need to auto-free. The main flows of transport, commerce, trade, development, and nonprofit action come together to form a consensus that integrates the stakeholders' short- and long-term interests in the region. Reducing pavement by 1% per year is one option. Unused parking lots and lanes can be converted into bikeways, walkways, parks, and playgrounds. Changes can emerge from the top down and the bottom up as people define the means and ends that fit the neighborhood. The city can offer suggestions, designs, tax breaks, and other incentives for people to walk, bicycle, and use transit.

Sustaining Transport with Sustainable Development

Auto-free design is impossible without thoughtful, relevant, and appropriate development. Designs from other cities worldwide that have implemented progressive designs may be an excellent place to start, as well as designs from cities that have never had automobiles. While high-density development is a way to think about auto-free infrastructure, lower densities are also possible. The design of the means for people to move themselves and objects using the most sustainable means and ends should be defined by the stakeholders and designers inside and outside of government. Sustainable development, which balances economic goals with long-term environmental viability, must be a part of this equation. Until transportation and development resonate sustainably, regions will be headed toward dangerous ecological consequences.

Integrating the Opposition

A challenge is to integrate the auto industry and car users to adapt to sustainable modes of transport. For auto-free design to work, these people must be a part of the process. The public, private, and nonprofit sectors can facilitate the transition to use less fossil fuel. Car companies can make electric or fuel cells or other types of vehicles that are more sustainable. Ideally, the automakers would seize the opportunity to develop sustainable transport infrastructure. Transit buses, rail cars, and person-powered vehicles are needed to move the next generations of citizens. Roads, parking lots, and pavement can be converted to relevant and appropriate land uses as defined by the stakeholders in the area.

The more people embrace practical, relevant, appropriate, and necessary action, the more everyone will gain.

Unified Support for Sustainable Transport

Of course, little, if anything, will happen without a concerted effort from politicians, media, corporations, nonprofits, religious groups, and the public. Making all this real may be a long shot or an inevitable consequence of progressive thought and action as weather patterns begin to dictate what happens. Global warming and climate change are rapidly threatening large amounts of infrastructure. To withstand extreme weather, governments must prepare. Unfortunately, most buildings were set up according to obsolete building codes that locate electrical meters, gas meters, water pumps, and heating and cooling equipment in basements where flooding can destroy them. This is one example. If buildings flood and are severely damaged, repairing them may take a long time, sometimes 5-10 or twenty years. If people don't live in an area, the transport infrastructure isn't used and may be ignored, like a damaged building.

Chapter 2
10 Points on Sustainable Transportation

1. Sustainable Transport and Development

A sustainable transport and development plan integrates infrastructure for walking, bicycling, and using transit with mixed-use development that allows people to meet needs within walking distance or a short transit ride. One goal is to provide the means for people to choose to live without using an automobile. Integrating transport and development into a regional plan allows cities/regions to situate Auto Free Designs into relevant and appropriate areas. Reducing auto use while expanding infrastructure for people to walk, bicycle, and use transit is a step in the right direction. Sustainable infrastructure is made with appropriate materials using processes that minimize damage to the environment, plants, animals, and people while generating jobs that sustain the community.

2. SAFETY

Over 44,000 people die each year in vehicle accidents, and hundreds of thousands are injured. Most people know a friend, relative, or neighbor who has been killed or severely injured in an auto accident. Some are permanently disabled, while many relive car accidents over and over. Other options that can make transportation safer are available for many people. Transit, driven by professional drivers, is safer, less expensive, and more efficient. If we reduce auto use and pavement while increasing transit, bicycling, walking and implementing traffic calming measures, we can reduce the chances that a vehicle will injure or kill pedestrians. Healthcare costs could be reduced if auto use is reduced. Traffic calming, which reduces the speed and intensity of traffic, can reduce the number and frequency of accidents and make the neighborhood more pleasant.

Unsafe Any Time Anywhere

The transportation system can't protect people from automobile accidents, and people who drive well can never be safe from unsafe drivers. The automobile transportation system exposes too many people to unnecessary risk. It's less secure than riding transit or riding a commercial airplane. Political leaders seeking to become famous can begin by making the city safer by reducing auto use and increasing infrastructure for sustainable transportation (walking, bicycling, and transit use) and sustainable development.

Modal Conflict, Separating Transport Modes

Mixing motorized and non-motorized transportation exposes pedestrians and bicycle users to the dangers of motorized transport. Separating transport functions and prioritizing pedestrians, bicyclers, and transit users may improve safety while incentivizing motorized transport to use other methods.

3. Environment

Automobiles pollute the air, land, water, atmosphere, plants, animals, and people. Large amounts of pollutants are released throughout automobile manufacturing, distribution, use, and disposal. This pollution concentrates locally and disperses globally. Groundwater is damaged when rain washes, gas, oil, brake fluid, transmission fluid, and other pollutants from the pavement into the lakes and streams. Tanks at gas stations, industrial sites, and homes leak into the soil and groundwater. Vehicle emissions accumulate in the atmosphere, which increases global warming.

Holistic Evaluation

Evaluating a system requires a look at all the parts of a system. The automobile system includes streets, highways and freeways, bridges, tunnels, and a vast infrastructure to maintain and operate. It's complex, profound, and has served people well, but not without a price. This infrastructure requires vast resources, equipment, and labor that could be used for other functions. Given all these inputs, it's essential to maximize the use of the existing system while creating the conditions for different ways to move people and goods without using so many inputs. This movement toward sustainable transport and development could generate positive consequences for society.

Climate Change: Adapt or Die

According to scientists, consequences of global warming include that the frequency and intensity of storms will increase, and sea levels will rise as polar ice packs melt. Already, we have seen islands with people disappear, and storms kill and injure large numbers of people and destroy the infrastructure that sustains them. While we can't say that global warming caused this or that storm directly, scientists have noted that global warming increases the chances of extreme weather patterns and destabilizes the climate that sustains us. As the climate becomes less stable, more people will lose the means to live. For these reasons, it's essential to consider and implement alternatives to auto use, which reduce pollution while providing the infrastructure for people to move in safer, healthier, and more sustainable ways.

4. Transit Oriented Design

Transit-oriented design locates transit stops within areas of high-density infrastructure that support many people. One model locates shops, restaurants, and clinics on the first floor and apartments on the top floors. Buildings that support large numbers of people may require more services to sustain those people. When this happens, more businesses, shops, and clinics can be located in a smaller area, which may generate adequate population density to justify mass transit. This creates the conditions for people to live without an automobile. Transit-oriented design is the opposite of a system of development located around freeways. Auto-oriented development locates development around a freeway exit, while transit-oriented development locates development around a transit stop. Transit-oriented design is more compatible with auto-free zones than freeway-oriented development. Auto-free cities design the main frame of the transport system around mass transit that is integrated into a mixed-use development.

5. Regional Planning

Regional planning integrates the transportation systems of sprawling development and small towns into large cities. Coordinated, region-wide transport is more convenient for passengers, more efficient than auto use, and beneficial for the region's economic, cultural, and social vitality. When large cities began, small towns were too far from the city to justify integration. As cities grew, some smaller towns were integrated into the city, and some were left independent. Low-density development around freeway exits offered construction jobs and tax revenue for the city, which was reduced by the city's money invested in infrastructure and tax reductions. As development is located around freeway exits, many developments still need to integrate transit into development. People without vehicles have long waits, long walks, and poor service. Providing mobility for people without cars can mean the difference between having a job and not having a job, getting a better education or staying at home, meeting with friends and relatives or talking to them on the phone, making it to the hospital on time, or dying along the way. Regional planning integrates small towns, sprawling development, and outlying areas into one transit system that should provide transport service to all who need it.

6. Long Range Planning.

Long-range planning, 20-30-50 years, can facilitate making significant changes gradually. The transition from an auto-oriented infrastructure to one that relies on walkways, bike lanes, and transit can be done in ways that minimize stressful changes in people. Implementing a 25-year plan that crosses generations and shifts in political climates is an excellent challenge for those who want to make a better city/region. A group of people from different sectors of society, including governments, universities, nonprofits, media, co-ops, and interested people, could be guardians of the implementation of auto-free ideas. The goal is to ensure that narrow political and economic interests uphold the long-term sustainable transportation and development plan. The plan should include periodic goals, perhaps every five years, establishing essential benchmarks. Funding could come from taxes on activities that pollute the environment or make people less healthy. Reducing auto use, infrastructure, and subsidies while increasing infrastructure for walking, bicycling, and transit can make the region more sustainable. Developing and implementing long-term plans for sustainable transportation and development is a way to improve the viability of a city/region. As cities/regions begin to implement Auto Free Designs, the health and safety of citizens may improve. Cities that pay attention to the consequences of globalization realize that they compete with cities worldwide for business, tourism, and the costs of running a city. Cities that produce real value for money will be more competitive nationally and worldwide. As cities mature, they may realize the benefits of person-powered transport: walking, bicycling, skateboarding, and rollerblading.

7. Reducing Auto Use

Reducing vehicle use could be a high priority for businesses, governments, and citizens. Congested highways, global warming, and car accidents undermine the value of driving. Automobiles require an extensive and comprehensive network of roadways to function. These roadways occupy large amounts of public space, cost billions to build and maintain, reduce areas for plants, animals, people, and buildings, and generate large amounts of pollution and heat in the summertime. Compared to walking, bicycling, and transit, automobiles use large amounts of resources and cause excessive pollution. Stress from congested highways has led to road rage and empty, hopeless resignation for commuters around the United States. Less auto use could reduce delivery times, congestion, emergency response times, fuel consumption, accidents, and deaths and injuries from auto accidents. As auto use is reduced, the city can remove or reallocate road space for other transport and development functions in the public interest.

8. Auto Free Infrastructure

Auto-free infrastructure combines sustainable transport and development in ways that allow people to meet their needs locally and sustainably. Making small changes in the transportation and development infrastructure that enable people to walk to meet needs is one way to create auto-free areas. If cities/regions have a long-term plan, they can make gradual changes, making the process more pleasant. If people can walk, bicycle, or take a short transit ride to go where they want, they may reduce car use. Walkways and bike lanes could provide safe, direct, and pleasant access to transit, shops, workplaces, parks, and clinics. To supply enough people to use transit, the buildings can be mixed-use, multistory buildings with shops, restaurants, and services on the first floor and apartments on the top floors. If a city integrates an Auto Free Zone around a transit stop, university, or center of a city, more land will be available for non-transportation functions. This land could be converted into public space, permaculture, or tasks that meet the needs of the people of the neighborhood. If it is converted to green space, it will reduce the Global Warming problem.

9. Auto Free Zones

An Auto Free Zone is an urban area that excludes auto use while providing walkways, bike lanes, and transit to move people and infrastructure for service vehicles. Walkways, bike lanes, transit, and buildings are situated in ways that allow people to meet their needs locally. Lanes for emergency, maintenance, construction, delivery, and transit vehicles are needed within an auto-free area to deliver services and goods and move people. Auto Free Zones give people the choice to live without an automobile. As a safer, healthier, more sustainable way to use the land, Auto Free Zones improve the quality of life in a neighborhood. Because people walk or bicycle instead of driving their cars, they exercise more, which can reduce health care needs and costs. University areas, the land around transit stops and city centers, and places around rivers, lakes, and waterways may be appropriate locations for auto-free zones. Auto Free Zones attract people, businesses, and nonprofits who seek to work, live, and play without the hazards, hassles, and pollution of automobiles. The air, land, water, plants, animals, and people are safer, healthier, and less stressed without the potential hazards and pollution of automobiles.

10. Auto-Free Cities

Cities before 1900 were auto-free, and now, a few cities, Venice, Italy, and areas of Fez, Morocco, operate without automobiles. The Arcosanti project is a project designed to minimize auto use. Auto-free cities move people and goods without using automobiles. The built environment is set up to facilitate walking, bicycling, and transit use. Delivery, emergency, utility, and maintenance vehicles use the streets. People, Pedi-cabs, delivery trucks, and modified transit vehicles can move cargo.

From Auto-Free Zones to Auto-Free Cities

Auto-free cities may start by expanding existing auto-free areas to the rest of the city. A master plan that lays out transit, bicycle, and walking corridors that integrate permaculture may complement expanding auto-free areas. This dual strategy from the inside out and outside in may provide significant practical options for cities to adapt. There are many beneficial consequences for people willing to enjoy the advantages of cities moving to reduce auto use.

Liberation from the Auto Plague

If people reduce auto use, many benefits may accrue. Since transit, walking, and bicycling require less money, the standard of living may increase. People will have more money to spend on non-transport functions. Money spent on automobiles may be used for other things. Land used for parking and car lanes may be used for community functions. With less auto use, pollution of the land, air, water, plants, animals, and people may be reduced, especially if one analyzes the whole cycle of production. As people walk, bicycle, and use transit, they may exercise more as they carry goods while enjoying their surroundings.

Freedom From the Automobile

Auto-free cities are a model of sustainable transportation and development. Implementing plans to build and maintain infrastructure, which allows people to move themselves and goods without automobiles, is a goal of Auto Free Cities. Providing walkways, bike lanes, and transit infrastructure while locating nonprofits, coops, and businesses in locations that allow people to meet needs within walking distance are ways for cities to provide people with the choice to live without automobiles.

Chapter 3
AFD Safety

Cities, states, and governments can't protect people from the transport system. Over 40,000 people are killed and six million injured in auto accidents every year. Another 64,000 people die from breathing toxic fossil fuel pollution from vehicles. Most accidents are caused by human error, but accidents would never happen without infrastructure. Fossil fuel vehicle use generates emissions that cause global warming. Climate change and global warming increase the frequency and intensity of storms. These storms kill and injure many people and destroy many buildings. The government, which regulates automobile production use and disposal, can't make the transport system safe. Small changes in the system generate small results. Little will change without a coherent, practical idea to change infrastructure and driving codes.

I Drive Everyday Without an Accident, What's the Problem?

How safe is our transportation system? If your house had gasoline exhaust coming in, would it be safe? Most people know a family or friend who has been killed or severely injured in a vehicle accident. Living in congested areas exposes people to more traffic, which can kill, injure, or poison you. Pollution from fossil fuel vehicles reduces air, land, and water quality. Roads and vehicular traffic dominate urban areas. Extreme profiteering and dominance by a few greedy clans produced vast urban areas that are unsafe for people to live in. With television, radio, and print ads blasting the comfort and convenience of auto use day and night, many passively accept these unsafe conditions, even as they put family and friends into a grave. Unless you don't drive or use the system, you must take extraordinary measures to avoid an accident. The following statistics show how dangerous these systems are. Statistics in this chapter come from the National Highway Traffic Safety Administration, the Insurance Institute for Highway Safety, and AAA's Foundation for Traffic Safety.

According to the World Health Organization

- 1.2 Million people die in road crashes every year.

- 50 Million are injured or disabled in car crashes every year.

- 50% of crash victims are pedestrians, bicyclers, and motorcycle drivers.

- 4% of GNP of each country is used up in vehicle crashes.

- Seat belt use reduced the risk of death by 61%.

- Child restraints can reduce childhood deaths by 35%.

- Helmets reduce injuries and fatalities by 45%.

- Enforcing drinking and driving laws reduces alcohol-related crashes by 20%.

- Reducing average speed by 1 kilometer per hour reduces crashes by 2%.

- Simple, low-cost engineering changes can save 1000s of lives every year.

In the United States

- 40,000 people die from road crashes every year.

- 2.35 Million are injured.

- 1,600 children under the age of 15 die each year.

- 8,000 people are killed per year by a driver between 16-20 years old.

- Crashes cost $230 billion per year to fix the damages to people, cars and buildings

- Road crashes are the highest cause of death for US citizens traveling abroad.

More Statistics on driving a car in the United States

- 95% of car crashes are from human error.

- 31% of drunk driving fatalities happen on the weekend.

- The highest numbers of drunk drivers are on the road between midnight and 3 am.

- Fatal crashes are four times more likely at night.

- Most car accidents happen within 25 miles of home.

- The most dangerous month is August.

- Saturday is the most dangerous day of the week.

- Speeding is a factor in 30% of fatal crashes.

- Drivers have a false sense of their ability to drive and multitask.

- Wear a seatbelt, focus on driving, and stay in control.

Air Pollution

Air pollution from vehicle exhaust is a serious health issue. Scientists blame soot for 64,000 premature deaths every year. Immediate effects of air pollution include eye irritation, throat irritation, and breathing problems. Ground-level ozone, toxic particles, and chemicals in polluted air can cause cancer, congenital disabilities, and nerve and brain damage. Air pollution can lead to difficulties with the respiratory, reproductive, neurological, and immune systems. Air pollution increases cancer and other chronic lung problems. Air-born soot from diesel engines causes respiratory issues. Soot trapped in the lungs can cause tissue damage and make existing lung problems worse. As soot settles into the lungs, bacterial infections and lung diseases slowly kill people. Studies show that heart attacks, irregular heartbeats, strokes, and heart failures are more frequent in areas with high levels of diesel soot.

The Media

Car commercials promote car use but rarely warn people about the dangers of driving. What people experience is quite different from what's advertised on TV. Even if people avoid auto accidents, they have to face other problems, which can jeopardize their safety. Racial profiling occurs when police stop people of color and harass, intimidate, and throw them in jail. Poor people who must use automobiles to meet needs struggle to make enough money to operate vehicles. If their car breaks down, gets a traffic violation, or gets caught without car insurance, they may lose their driving privileges.

Automakers Resist Safety Regulations

Automakers resist regulations to make their vehicles safer. Even though they may be able to sell more cars that way, they fight what reduces profits. So, the government is supposed to ensure the infrastructure is safe, but this has proven impossible. Self-driving vehicles could make a difference, but when people drive or do anything, they make mistakes. When the mistakes have deadly consequences, it's a severe problem. Because the infrastructure is so vast, the job of changing it is beyond most people's imagination. So now we have this extensive infrastructure; some are obsolete, some are dangerous, and some need maintenance.

Society Pushes Unsafe Auto Use

The main forces of society, the state, corporations, and media push people to buy, maintain, and dispose of automobiles, even though we should be reducing auto use. The auto industry provides jobs, but now we are only in a position to accept economic activity if we consider the environmental consequences.

Why do we need Auto Free Design Safety?

Over 40,000 people die from car accidents, and over 3.2 million are injured every year in the US. Most people know a friend or relative who was killed by a car. Often, the emotional pain can last for years. That pain can strike people who were not in the accident. In a few seconds, someone is alive, and the next, they are dead. You may be able to control your driving, but you can't manage what others do. With some planning and good habits, you can reduce your risk of an accident. The system is deadly, and another design could make transport much safer. Expanding areas for walking, using bicycles, and transit may increase transport safety.

Fossil Fuel Vehicle Use Destroys People, Plants and Animals

Exhaust from internal combustion engines burning fossil fuels destroys people, plants, and animals. Pavement is death for plants and animals. Land covered with asphalt and concrete gets no light, air, or water. Covering the earth with pavement is like living under a tarmac. Roadkill is common in cities and countries. It's a brutal system that gives the highest priority to the automobile. You can kill someone with a car, and rarely are there any consequences. The laws shield people from liability for killing and injuring people, plants, and animals with vehicles.

A Bit of History: How did we get here?

The current system, the roads, and freeways were made when oil seemed limitless and pollution harmless. One assumption was that driving a car is better than walking, riding a bicycle, or using transit. Why walk or bicycle in the rain, snow, and cold when you can open a car door, turn the key, and ride pleasantly? We are not in the Stone Age. Why does something painful like walking when you can drive? Also, cars provide mobility; just get in your car and go to the other side of the country. The fantasy of freedom and independence was mechanized in the form of an automobile. Another assumption was common: The car should have priority over all other forms of transport. Bike lanes were not necessary because no one would want to ride one. Some suburban areas need sidewalks. Roads and cars made bicycles a thing of the primitive past. Why walk or take transit if you can ride with style, comfort, and pleasure with your vehicle? For generations, a measure of success was whether or not meat was served for every meal. Cars and vehicles have a similar stature. If you have them, why not use them? There are no disadvantages.

European Cities With Less Corruption Improved Transport

Safety By Increasing Infrastructure for Non-Motorized Transport

In some European countries like Germany, Netherlands, and Belgium, where the oil lobby is not so solid and social democracies, they recognized the value of a transport system that prioritizes pedestrian, bicycle, and transit use. They make bike lanes, restrict car use in the central city, and make transit more accessible. The Europeans were doing this in the 80s and 90s. Eventually, when Bloomberg became the Mayor of New York City, the priorities of the transportation system began to shift from cars to pedestrians, bicyclers, and transit users.

Low Density and Congestion Reduce Safety

The low density of most American cities makes walking, bicycling, and using transit more difficult, dangerous, and often impossible. As congestion increases, travel time increases for emergency vehicles, which can make the difference between life and death. Traffic jams increase the stress on commuters and generate road rage, which can get violent. For low-income people in suburbia, the cost of driving a vehicle can reduce money for housing, healthcare, education, food, and clothing. With less money and fewer options to walk, bicycle, or use transit, people with low incomes may drive unsafe or illegal cars.

Even Though Only 25% of People in Manhattan Own a Car, Traveling is Quite Dangerous.

In Manhattan, New York City, 25% of the people own cars. With ample transit, bike lanes, taxis, and sidewalks, many enjoy the pleasures of living without a vehicle. Population density makes it easy for people to get to and from popular destinations. You can travel easily to a restaurant, park, garden, or desired destination. High density makes it easier to live without a car. If you add the problems of owning a car in Manhattan, such as difficult parking, traffic jams, and many regulations, most people live without a vehicle. If people can choose to live without a vehicle, they will. For most people in Manhattan, living without a car is far more pleasant than owning a car.

Safety in Manhattan in Auto-Free Stuyvesant Town

Some cities, including New York City, have developments with limited car use. Stuyvesant town is one of them. Developed after WW II for veterans, the private project, funded by Metropolitan Life Insurance, was criticized for not allowing people of color, reducing public space, and using eminent domains for personal purposes. The idea was to enable people to live in a park-like setting in a dense urban area. The project has a few roads going through, but only a little traffic. With trees, fountains, and playgrounds, the area is less urban with more green space. Without stores, emergency vehicles, and large areas for parking, the area has less noise and pollution.

Transport System Produces and Exploits Victims

The transport system produces millions of victims per year. Treating people with injuries from vehicle accidents is a big business. Governments should be doing more to increase the safety of the transportation system, but economic pressure encourages people to keep the system going. Since the privatization of healthcare, the price of health care has increased dramatically. While the healthcare industry does not advocate for more victims, they make big money from the victims of car crashes. The victims pay for the insurance and the healthcare industries profit from it.

Pedestrian Victims

Over 5,000 pedestrians die each year, and over 70,000 are injured. People below the age of sixteen and over seventy are the most vulnerable. Children between the ages of 5 and 9 suffer high rates of death and injury. Males make up 68% of pedestrian deaths. In 2002, 36% of pedestrians in a fatal pedestrian/car crash had a blood alcohol level above 08%. Most pedestrian fatalities happen between 6 and 9 pm on a Friday or Saturday night. The highest number of vehicle accidents with pedestrians occur at non-intersection locations. Pedestrians are more likely to be killed in a rural vehicle crash. When cars make left and right turns at intersections, pedestrians are at a higher risk than turn-restricted intersections (no right-hand turns on a red light in Manhattan). Over 1/3 of all pedestrian-vehicle crash fatalities involve people over the age of 70. Slower walking, reduced vision, hearing, and reaction times are some of the reasons for the high death rates.

Media and Reality

Car commercials promote car use but rarely warn people about the dangers of driving. What people experience is quite different from what's advertised on TV. Even if people avoid accidents, they face other problems that can jeopardize their safety. Poor people, who must use automobiles to meet their needs, struggle to make enough money to keep their vehicles. If their car breaks down, gets a traffic violation, or gets caught without insurance, they could lose their driver's license. Living without a vehicle generates many problems in some areas when people can't get to work, school, or stores. Without a car, they can't meet family needs. With the current minimum wage and transportation system requirements, people are caught in difficult circumstances.

Transport System Functions as a Police Dragnet for People of Color and People of Difference

Racist police increase the danger. Police stop people of color int, intimidate them, and throw them in jail without probable cause. People of color and low-income white people rarely have money to pay for a well-functioning vehicle. If you have a tail light out or some other minor problem, the police can pull you over and harass you, give you a ticket, and provoke an incident that could get you beat up or killed or face fines and imprisonment. If you are white but don't conform to what is considered "normal," which includes punks, hippies, artists, and others, you are a police magnet. The logic seems to be since you don't look straight, you must be doing something wrong. For people of difference, the transport system is a ticket to problems with police that may lead to loss of license, vehicle, injuries, lawsuits, and death.

Safety Belts and Driving Habits

To increase your chances of surviving a rollover accident, the National Highway and Traffic Safety Administration recommends wearing safety belts and avoiding panic reactions when driving. When drivers panic, they overcompensate by turning the steering wheel too far, too fast, and losing control. 75% of rollovers happen on undivided highways and rural areas, so extra precautions are needed. Other car maintenance issues reduce driver safety. Worn and improperly inflated tires increase the risk of an accident. Loading a vehicle with too much weight on the roof or one side can also increase the risk of a rollover crash. 15 person passenger vans are more dangerous than cars. Between 1990 and 2001, over a thousand people died in 15 passenger van accidents.

Safety in Rural Areas

Rural roads pose significant challenges for driver safety. People drive more when there is less traffic and have more accidents. Many intersections have no stop signs, and others have signs, but they need to be set up better. Sometimes, people don't realize how close the intersection is and can't stop before the stop sign. Tight curves, snow, ice, or gravel on the pavement make the roads slippery and dangerous. The lack of traffic can lull people into a false sense of safety, especially when approaching slow-moving farm vehicles. Adding a horse and buggy to the equation makes the area more dangerous.

Global Warming and Transport Safety

Global warming reduces the safety of the transport system. Fossil fuel emissions produce carbon dioxide, which increases the temperature of the earth. As temperatures rise and climate destabilizes, extreme weather increases the number of accidents and reduces the safety of the transport system. Global warming reduces the safety of the transport system by:

• Increasing heat waves that soften, distort, and destroy asphalt.

• Flooding, storm surges, hurricanes, and tsunamis that damage and destroy roads, tunnels, subways, and bridges.

• Disrupting traffic, delaying construction, and undermining the foundations of transport infrastructure.

• High winds blow down trees and power lines, which stops traffic.

• Hurricanes wash out and flood streets, making them impassible.

• Tornadoes wipe out bridges and damage roads.

Priorities of a Transport System

Safety is a priority for a transport system. If people can walk, bicycle, or use transit without vehicle threats, they may be safer than using a car. A lot depends on the infrastructure, or how much road space is for vehicles and how much is for non-motorized transport. More space for vehicles is often less safe for non-motorized transport. Usually, walking, bicycling, and transit infrastructure are safer than infrastructure dominated by auto use. Moving people and objects in a safe, pleasant, and efficient way is a priority for a transport system. As global warming intensifies, it becomes clear that reducing fossil fuel use is critical if we want a safer transport system.

Infrastructure and Safety

Infrastructure determines the safety of a transport system. Imagine areas of the city without automobiles or minimal use. Fewer people would be killed and injured. Less pavement and traffic could increase safety in many areas. Cities with fewer paved areas to design, build, maintain, and operate may be safer and more pleasant than cities with more roads. Infrastructure for pedestrians, bicyclers, and transit users may use less energy and money to design, build, maintain, and operate, especially when the cost of air, land, and water pollution is added to the equation. Less tax money would be needed for roads, regulations, and adjudication. If you build excellent highways, people tend to fill them. What if you make bike lanes instead? What if those bike lanes give you the advantage over a car to reach your destination? One standard model in Europe is to develop city centers for non-motorized traffic while limiting auto use to the boundaries of urban areas.

Sustainable Transport is Safer

As auto use is reduced, transit, walkways, and bikeways can be improved so that more people can move safely. With an infrastructure that makes non-motorized transport the safest, fastest, and cheapest way to get around, car users will choose to walk, cycle, and ride transit. To increase transport safety, cities can expand infrastructure for walking, bicycling, and using transit. If people can walk, bicycle, or use transit to meet their needs in auto-free areas, they can live with less fear and stress, trying to avoid a vehicle accident.

Auto-Free Zones and Safety

One way to increase transportation safety is to develop auto-free zones. These areas, which exclude the use of automobiles, provide safer transportation without automobiles. A combination of buses, delivery trucks, emergency vehicles, and construction and maintenance vehicles can serve and maintain these areas. These areas, which offer people a choice to live without cars, are safer, healthier, and have less vehicle noise. Within a car-free zone, shops, clinics, markets, and workplaces are located a short walk, bike, or transit ride away.

As the infrastructure shifts to include walkways, bike lanes, and transit, people will enjoy a higher quality of life with less pollution. With good design, the movement of pedestrians, cyclists, and transit can create a visual and aesthetic dynamic. As people exercise more, they need less health care and fewer drugs. Since the city would not have to build, maintain, and patrol streets, the city could offer tax breaks to neighborhoods that reduce pavement and create auto-free zones. Without traffic and pollution, people will live with less danger. As the beauty, style, and grace of these areas draw people in, people will see the benefits and want to live in auto-free areas.

1001 Innovations

Since oil monopolies put a stranglehold on innovation and design in the transport industry, the shining moment of human ingenuity passed, and those with skill, talent, and motivation gave up on their fabulous dreams. Such is the case with the transport industry and many others. To maximize profit, all competition had to be eliminated. When designs for electric or other vehicles surfaced, car companies would buy the patent to ensure it never challenged their economic territory. If cities implement auto-free zones, people, groups, and businesses can create innovative ways to move people and objects without using vehicles. This will encourage people to use people power to move themselves and objects. This could improve the health of people.

Need for a Vision With Hope

People may succumb to apathy and despair without a holistic vision of a viable alternative. A vision generates hope. People see how it can improve their lives. Freedom from the danger and pollution of the auto-oriented transport system can reduce the apathy, stress, and oppressive conditions of the transport system.

Progressive Priorities

A progressive transport system provides infrastructure for people to move safely without owning a vehicle. Increasing infrastructure for walking, bicycling, and using transit may increase transport safety. As people walk, bicycle, and use transit more, they get more exercise and require less health care. Areas without vehicles may be safer. Fewer people will be killed or injured from vehicle accidents. If pavement is reduced, more land will be available for plants and animals. If people drive less, walk, bicycle, or use transit, the transport system may become safer with less toxic pollution.

The Government Has Failed to Protect People

Auto Free Design

City, state, and federal governments can't protect people from the consequences of the auto-oriented transport system. Over 40,000 people die, and 2 million are injured in auto accidents every year. Another 64,000 people die from breathing air pollution. Auto use generates emissions, which damage and kill living things and the environment. The Greenhouse effect, which kills people while destroying buildings, neighborhoods, and villages, increases extreme weather patterns and destabilizes the climate. The government, which regulates the production, use, and disposal of automobiles, can't make driving safe. One solution is sustainable transport, which increases infrastructure for walking, bicycling, and using transit.

Chapter 4
AFD Why

1. Fossil Fuel Use Emits Toxins That Destroy Life

Vehicles that burn gasoline produce toxic smoke that kills and injures all life, including people, plants, and animals. Fossil fuel emissions increase the intensity of global warming, which destabilizes the climate and makes storms more frequent and intense. With global warming, heat waves will become more prolonged and more intense. Sea levels will rise, and flooding and storm surges will generate more catastrophes. Human activities will become more difficult as the earth becomes less and less habitable. With Auto Free Design, people will walk, bicycle, and use transit more, and this reduces fossil fuel emissions.

2. Auto Auto-free areas Have Fewer Deaths and Injuries from Vehicle Crashes

Close to 100,000 people die each year from vehicle crashes and vehicle pollution, and 3 million are injured. Reducing these numbers will decrease the pain and suffering caused by vehicle accidents. Even with improvements to road design and traffic signals, the system is unsafe. As pavement is reduced or eliminated, fewer pedestrians and bicyclers will come in contact with vehicles. With less threat from vehicles, fewer people will die from vehicle crashes. Related costs will go down as people pay less for burial costs and medical treatment for those who are killed or injured.

3. Vehicle Exhaust Kills People, Plants and Animals

Vehicles emit toxic smoke, which kills people, plants and animals. Carbon monoxide is a colorless, odorless gas that slows people down and takes their lives away. Sulfur dioxide mixes with water to make sulfuric acid. Other toxic chemicals do similar things in gasoline-they injure and kill people.

4. To Reduce Noise

Transport noise reduces the quality of life. People can't have a conversation with sirens blaring, tires screeching, and motors roaring. Excessive noise devalues the urban environment, reduces property values, and makes people want to leave. Pleasant sounds are snuffed out. People can't hear the guitar, can't hear the person on the phone, and can't enjoy a peaceful moment. Vehicle noise reduces the quality of life, increases stress, and makes a quiet, pleasant life impossible. People can't hear birds singing, people playing, or making music. As auto-free areas expand, sound is liberated from the assault of the machine.

5. To Make More and Better Habitat for People, Plants and Animals.

Auto-free areas require less pavement. Less pavement makes more land free to breathe, get wet, and support plants, animals, and people. Plants replace the pavement. Plants clean, invigorate and make the air, land, and water viable. With proper management and planning, urban areas connect with rural areas to increase habitat for plants and animals. Reducing pavement generates benefits that improve the quality of life as more land is available for plants and animals to grow and thrive.

6. Using Human Power To Move People and Goods Generates Advantages

As people walk, bicycle, and use transit, they exercise more. Exercising makes people feel better and reduces health care costs. Person-powered transport generates more opportunities for people to connect with people, plants, and animals, share culture, and support community activities. Walking and bicycling use less energy and are more efficient. Human-powered transport frees people from the oppressive consequences of auto use. As people learn to walk and bicycle, they increase their freedom from the oppressive conditions of vehicle use.

7. To Free People from the Stress of Vehicle Ownership

Vehicle ownership is stressful. You must get a driver's license, buy and insure a vehicle, drive properly, maintain the vehicle, and know how to avoid problems with the police. For people with limited incomes who must drive to get to work, school, or meet needs, owning a car to live is oppressive. You must choose to pay for necessities that you can't afford because the vehicle eats up the budget. With less money for a car, people don't get insurance, fix the door properly, or drive with a driver's license; this quickly jeopardizes their future when they get tickets from the police or have an accident.

8, Sustainable Transport Is More Efficient

Walking, bicycling, and transit use require less energy than vehicle use. Walking and bicycling uses no fossil fuels and buses and trains are more efficient than vehicles. The sun, wind, or other clean fuels can power electric buses, trains, and subways. Bicycles are the most energy-efficient way to move people. A 15-pound bicycle can move a 200-pound person. A car is 4,000 pounds. So moving a car requires many times the energy of a bicycle. An empty bus is less efficient than a car with one person. A bus requires 7 or 8 people to become more efficient than a car.

9. Sustainable Transport is Better for the Air, Land, and Water

Sustainable transport requires fewer vehicles if people walk, cycle, and use transit more than driving. This reduces air pollution. Since less land is needed for vehicles, less land will have to be paved. Unpaved areas can support plant growth, which improves the soil, produces oxygen, and uses carbon dioxide. Plants can be grown for food, medicine, and pleasure. Vehicles drip less gas, oil, and toxic fluids onto the pavement as less pavement is made and maintained. These poisonous fluids flow into the storm sewer and contaminate local waterways. Cities gain enormously if there's less infrastructure to design, build, maintain, police, and adjudicate.

10. Sustainable Transport Supports People, Plants and Animals

If people live without vehicles, they have more time for other things. Infrastructure for non-motorized transport requires less time, energy, money, and resources to design, build, maintain, police, and adjudicate than auto-oriented transport. Without cars to buy, maintain, park, license, and wash, people have more time to walk, bicycle, and ride transit. With fewer paved areas, there's more room to grow plants that clean and nourish the air, land, and water. People who walk and bicycle get more exercise, which can reduce the need for health care.

11. Producing Vehicle Infrastructure Generates Large Amounts of Fossil Fuel Emissions

Roads, bridges, and tunnels require large amounts of energy to design, build, and operate. Most of that energy comes from fossil fuels. Infrastructure is made of steel, concrete, and asphalt. These materials are very heavy and require large machines and fuel-intensive processes. Producing, maintaining, and repairing bridges, tunnels, and roads require large amounts of fossil fuel, time, energy, and money.

12. When People Don't Own a Car, They Have More Time to Do Other Things

For many, paying for a vehicle requires working a lot of time per month. In 2017, the typical monthly cost per household for vehicle use was $700 per month. If you make $50,000 annually, your weekly net income is close to $750. So that's one week per month working to pay for a vehicle. Living without a car means you have more time. You would still have to pay for transit, which is less than $250 per month. If you live close to the means to meet needs, you need less money and should have more time. Sleeping, reading, writing, and other activities may be possible in transit. Usually, you can relax more because you are not driving.

13. Dense Urban Areas Allow People to Walk to Meet Needs

With taller buildings and compact designs, cities can be set up to meet needs and wants without traveling far. With many people in a small area, the store, museum, school, or hospital is often a short distance away. Walking, riding a bicycle, or using transit for short distances can be pleasant, affordable, refreshing, and more challenging in the rain and snow. Transit may take more time, but that time may be used to eat, sleep, socialize, read, or write. It also takes discipline, especially on a crowded subway. High-density infrastructure, which typically has more buildings and transit for a city block, can make it easier for people to meet needs and wants within walking distance without the burden of owning a vehicle.

14. A Streamlined Transport System Helps Cities Adapt to Global Warming

Auto-free design reduces transport infrastructure. People and bicycles are smaller than vehicles and require less pavement. As Global Warming intensifies, more transport infrastructure will be at risk. Forward-leaning cities can prioritize which infrastructure to strengthen to withstand global warming forces and which to let deteriorate. A long-term plan may reduce pavement and increase walkways, bike paths, and transit. Pavement may be recycled, and land used to make sustainable transport infrastructure. Walk and bikeways may reduce required infrastructure. With intelligent design, it may be possible to pave only the faster, high-traffic bike lanes. If local materials were used to build infrastructure, responding and rebuilding may be less work after a significant weather event.

15. Auto-Free Design Improves the Standard of Living

In 2018, households spent $700 per month to use a car. For many, this equals about 25% of their income if they make $50,000 annually. High transport costs increase the cost of living and reduce the standard of living, especially for people with less income. When people drive, they exercise less, reducing their health, which decreases their standard of living. If I'm not paying for a car, I have more money to spend on other things. I may have to spend money on transit or a bicycle, but this is less than the cost to buy, maintain, use, and dispose of a vehicle. If people spend less money on transport, they will have more money to spend on housing, food, and other things. This can boost the economy, especially if most auto-related businesses are large corporations that extract wealth from the local economy.

16. Sustainable Transport Increases Transport Choices

If you live in an urban area with good transit and can walk to meet your needs, it may be a challenge to imagine what it's like to live in an area where you must have a car. The opposite is probably true. If you live in the country, it may be a challenge to imagine living where you can walk to buy food, eat at a restaurant, or go to work. With effort, people using a vehicle can reduce or eliminate driving by walking, cycling, or using transit. Careful planning may reduce miles traveled. Transit requires more time but offers benefits that save time and money. I can sleep, eat, read, write, and talk to people in transit. If I'm driving, this is impossible. As people change their transportation habits, many benefits accrue. Walking, bicycling, and transit often generate more exercise than driving a car. With some skill and ingenuity, combining, minimizing, and eventually eliminating vehicle trips is possible.

17. Using Sustainable Methods is More Efficient Use of Land and Infrastructure

Fewer vehicles require less roads and infrastructure, which can significantly reduce transport costs. Think about what a government does. They must design, engineer, produce, regulate, and maintain highways and infrastructure to keep all users safe. They must do this correctly, or they can be sued. That's a tremendous amount of work, requiring time, energy, and money. Our tax dollars pay for this. With less pavement, transit users and taxpayers benefit.

18. Sustainable Transport Makes People More Free

When people own a vehicle, their transport requires more work. To own a car, you must find and buy the right vehicle and ensure it is safe to drive. You must insure the car, register it with the state, and follow all the rules. You must fill it with gas, oil, antifreeze, brake fluid, and air. Once this is finished, you can drive it, but you must know and follow the rules correctly, or you could get in trouble with the law. Now, if you walk, bicycle, or use transit, you have much less work. Walking requires preparing for the elements, which most people do anyway. Bicycling requires money for a bicycle, or if you're intelligent with tools and bikes, you can make your own for a small price. Transit involves a bit of practice but is easier than riding a bicycle. Sustainable transport, walking, bicycling, and using transit, does not require large amounts of money upfront, no license, no collision or liability insurance, little training, and much less risk. Bicycling is dangerous when sharing the road with vehicles. The whole point is that sustainable transport gives you more time, money, and safety.

19. Sustainable Transport Requires Less Parking Infrastructure

Walking, bicycling, and using transit require less infrastructure than using vehicles. Think of the parking spaces that wouldn't be needed if we reduced the number of cars by 10%. That's a lot of pavement that would not have to be engineered, produced, installed, and maintained. How much space does a bicycle require compared to a car? Yes, transit requires significant infrastructure that is quite expensive initially. Still, the cost per person per mile traveled is less than using a vehicle and generates more environmental benefits than vehicles.

20. To Reduce Pain and Suffering from Vehicle Accidents

Vehicle use is quite dangerous. Many people, plants, and animals are killed and injured every day in vehicle accidents. The cost of medical care for people injured in vehicle accidents is quite high. If someone dies, people have to pay to have them buried, which can spell economic disaster, especially if they have no life insurance. If a person in the house or apartment dies, the household may lose the deceased person's income. This can spiral people into economic disasters that make people homeless. Emotional pain and suffering can impact people for many years, sometimes a lifetime, and beyond.

21. To Make a Better Life

People who spend time making money to buy, use, and dispose of a vehicle often have less time than people who walk, bicycle, or use transit. With some planning and practice, a bike can make short trips easily. Parking is free, and some buses and subways allow bicycles. Combining a bicycle with transit can generate significant advantages. Bike to the subway or bus, and put it in transit, and when you get off, keep biking. When I arrive, I have the bicycle to ride quickly to my destination. As I ride, I get exercise, feel the streets and people, and wind up with more energy than when I started. Many variations are possible. I take it easy on the bus. I eat, sleep, write, and relax. I'm not wasting my time or using my time to transport myself. A bicycle usually requires full attention, but it feels effortless once you learn the fundamentals. For many people, living without a vehicle is a more active life with more time to do more pleasant things than working to own a car.

22. To Liberate People from Oppressive Conditions of the Transport System

For many people, an alternative to driving is impossible. When people must own a car to get to work, buy food, or go to school and can't afford it, life becomes quite difficult. It becomes a treadmill of crises. Without infrastructure that allows people to meet needs within walking distance, the transport system becomes oppressive, especially when race or difference is added to the equation. People of difference are people who look or act differently or are part of an uncommon subculture. As people work more for less money and pay more for everything, their ability to afford to live goes down. If you must own a vehicle, the time, money, and energy to buy, use, maintain, and license a vehicle may become quite oppressive.

23. Sustainable Transport Generates More Freedom

If you grew up in a culture that uses cars, walking, bicycling, and riding, transit may be a foreign notion. If you have never owned a car but used one, it probably needs to be made apparent how much effort it requires to own and operate a vehicle. In the right conditions, owning and using a car can be pleasant, but it can be oppressive for many people on lower incomes. For many, especially in Manhattan, NY, living without a car is a preference and advantage. People have more time to do other things without a car to park, maintain, license, and clean. There's more time to see a movie, read a book, or stroll through the park.

24. To Make a More Pleasant Place to Live

People who don't use vehicles, pedestrians, bicyclers, and transit users often breathe vehicle pollution, listen to loud transport sounds, and are stressed from fear of being hit by a vehicle. Most people have grown up in these conditions, and now these conditions feel normal and acceptable. A transportation system without vehicles is more pleasant. Without noise, pollution, accidents, and death, life becomes more enjoyable, and nature comes alive.

25. Vehicle Infrastructure Prevents Walking, Bicycling and Transit Use

A vehicle is required in many areas of the country. In these areas, walking, cycling, or using transit may be difficult or impossible. The infrastructure is set up for vehicles. Some areas have no sidewalks. Roads may be so narrow that bicycling is quite dangerous. Many places have no transit, or transit could be more efficient to use. Low-density infrastructure or urban areas with buildings less than two stories are typically spread so far apart that even with a vehicle, the distances take away from the pleasure of living.

26. Using Sustainable Methods is More Efficient for People

If I walk, bicycle, or use transit, I use less energy than a vehicle. Think about how much a person weighs and how much a car weighs. A person weighs 200 pounds. A vehicle weighs at least fifteen times that, or 3.000 pounds. Wow, how many people would be required to push that car around? A bicycle weighs 15 pounds and can move a person who is 300 pounds, so a bike can move a person who is 20 times as heavy. Moving a person by walking, bicycling, or using transit is almost always more efficient than using a car. Use that efficiency to your advantage. Why move that car around when you could move yourself or a bicycle?

27. Using Sustainable Transport is Healthier for People

When people walk, bicycle, and use transit, they use more human power than a vehicle. As people burn calories walking and bicycling, they become healthier than sitting in a car. Exercise provides more oxygen to the blood and makes people feel more alive. Transport infrastructure that facilitates personal power makes transport more sustainable. As more people use healthier, safer travel methods, healthcare costs may decrease.

28. Sustainable Transport is Better for Animals

Nothing grows on concrete and asphalt until people, plants, and animals break through to allow light, air, and water. Animals can live with plants but not with asphalt or concrete. As less pavement is required for transport, more land can be used to grow plants. Reducing pavement and vehicle use can make more land available for plants and animals. Imagine how much can be grown on one giant parking lot.

29. Sustainable Transport is Best for the Air, Land and Water

Reducing pavement by 1% per year generates many benefits. Unused car lanes can be phased out, and sustainable solutions can be phased in. Without an asphalt or concrete covering, land can breathe, get cleaned, and absorb nourishment from rain, roots, and plants. Plants purify the land, air, and water. The air becomes cleaner with less surface area covered with asphalt and vehicles pushing out vast amounts of pollution. People breathe less toxic vehicle emissions. Fewer people are damaged by poisonous vehicle smoke. With less pavement preventing plants from improving the air, land, and water quality, people can live a more pleasant life.

Chapter 5
AFD Philosophy of Design

What is Auto Free Design?

Auto Free Design reduces auto use while increasing infrastructure for non-motorized transport and transit. It develops land use and development patterns that provide the fastest, most efficient, and environmentally friendly way to move people. Auto Free Design integrates walkways, bike lanes, and transit into sustainable development. Walkways, bike lanes, and transit move people to and from high-density developments. Mixed-use development, which allows people to meet needs within walking distance, complements a rapid transit system of buses, trains, trams, and subways.

Auto Transport Reduces Advantages

Auto Free Design governs technology to move people and objects in ways that minimize damage to life and the environment. Auto-oriented transport undermines our ability to live. People spend too much time and money to drive a car. That time could be used to enjoy life, ride a bicycle, take transit, or walk. Fossil fuel vehicles generate 25% of emissions that cause Global Warming. As congestion threatens the value of auto use and the economy that depends on it, people will look for other options.

The Transport System is a Class System

Auto-oriented transport is a class-based system. People must own a vehicle to get to work, school, or visit a clinic but can't afford it because wages are too low. You must have enough money and be codified and trained to obey laws, pay bills, and drive correctly. Many urban areas don't have the infrastructure for walking, cycling, or using transit. People who can't drive are excluded. Many people without jobs can't afford a car. They may not be able to afford insurance, proper repairs, or to get a driver's license. The design of the system excludes participation. People who walk, bicycle, and use transit are killed and injured in vehicle crashes and must breathe toxic air from vehicles. They are victims of the vehicle transport system and are the solution to the problems of the auto-oriented transport system.

Oppressive Codes of Transport Destroy Freedom

Auto-free design facilitates living independently of structures of domination. Many codes, including family traditions, peer pressure, and media, direct people to use a car for transport. Buying, maintaining, insuring, licensing, disposing, and paying for a vehicle is expensive. Often, these codes favor people with money, people with white skin, or people who conform to the dominant reality. Low-income people usually buy cheap, old, beat-up cars to save money. These cars are police magnets. An officer sees a minor problem with the car, pulls them over, and the situation gets out of control, especially with poorly trained officers. The driver and passengers are beaten up and killed or charged with crimes they did not commit. If people don't own and use a car, they don't need to put time, money, stress, and energy into using a car or face the injustice of the system.

Auto Transport Leads to Eviction

People with less income struggle to afford a vehicle to take them to and from work. Often, the car they have is used and could break down any minute. In the winter, during heat waves and extreme weather, vehicles are more likely to break down. Families with two incomes and more than one job may need two cars. If their car breaks down, they won't be able to get to work, and often, they can't afford to fix it. At this point, the transport system becomes oppressive. If they miss workdays, they may lose their job. For many, no job means no money or rent, which means eviction. When people are evicted, they go into emergency crisis mode. In a city where transit is a priority, more people can get to work for less money and some have less stress about losing their housing.

High Cost of Convenience: Economic Servitude?

Have you ever had to fix a broken car and not have the money? We have accepted enormous amounts of pain and suffering to drive cars. Most people know someone who's been killed or seriously injured in a car crash. Hospital bills and burial expenses can destroy the economic integrity of a household. One must work to buy, maintain, and dispose of the car, follow the driving codes, look respectful to the police officer, fill the car with gas, pay the insurance bill, and watch over the car to make sure it won't break down or to make sure no one steals it. You must not fall asleep, drive drunk, or violate the codes of driving. These codes form people into an auto mold that stifles the free flow of desire and creativity.

Poverty and the Economic Drudgery of Owning a Vehicle

Many people can barely pay for healthcare, rent, and food, so a car can be a misery. If one has a cheap car, it can break down quickly, require costly repairs, and keep breaking down until you get rid of it. Some people drive marginal cars that could fall apart at any time. Old and broken cars are police magnets. If the police see that you don't fit the mold, a person of color, female, gay, not straight or punk, or not a straight white male, the suspicion goes up, and they look for things. Under police scrutiny, some people fear danger and respond accordingly, and the results may not be so good. Some end up in prison, hospital, or morgue. For too many people, having a car is a huge liability that could quickly destroy their world. What will you do if it breaks down and you don't have the money to fix it? If it breaks down far from home, you must take what you can find and hope for the best. If you are in an accident, your whole world could collapse.

The Commodification of Mind, Body and Automobile

Now, even if you have enough money to buy and maintain a car, the process domesticates and forms a person into patterns of ownership, consumption, and subservience. Owning a vehicle requires an ownership mindset. I can't share my car with other people. This will lead to problems with insurance and maintaining the vehicle. Insurance companies don't want other people driving my car. With ownership comes liability. You are thrust into the position of someone who could quickly kill someone because you are driving a vehicle. As people use automobiles, their minds are colonized by the private transport mentality, which requires locking vehicles to keep thieves away, insurance to minimize losses, and a mindset to control the commodity and to beware of traffic laws, police, and courts. If you walk, bicycle, or use transit, the experience may be quite different. You are not confined to the constraints of driving.

Infrastructure for Walking, Bicycling, and Using Transit Requires Less Infrastructure, Cost, and Regulation

Roads require vast expertise, energy, and materials to build, operate, and regulate. Taxes, fees, and fines pay for designing, building, maintaining, policing, and disposing of the infrastructure required to own and operate a vehicle. People spend a lot of time, energy, and money to use a vehicle. Walking and bicycling infrastructure requires less materials and methods to build and operate. If cities maximize people's power, they need less pavement.

The Trade-Off: Convenience for Sustainability

Some people may lose convenience, safety, and comfort if they can't drive a vehicle. Drivers would not be able to park adjacent to their destination, which is often the case now. Cars can be a significant advantage over walking, bicycling, and transit use in the cold, snow, and rain. With air conditioning, heating, and many other car comforts, people can isolate themselves from extreme weather. Automobiles can carry up to six people and goods at the same time. Not everyone gains from an auto-free system, but the long and short-term gains from less auto use offset the loss inconvenience. Also, people must remember that the current transportation system was optimized for vehicle use. Another system that prioritizes sustainable transport would not make using a vehicle the fastest, cheapest, most pleasant way to move to a destination. Fine-tuning the system could generate more luxurious ways to move people without using a car.

Increase Freedom with Auto-Free Design

Governments can increase freedom by providing the choice to live without an automobile. While reducing auto use, governments can design urban areas so that people can choose to own a car or not. Many urban areas require auto ownership by default. If you don't own a car, you can't get to work, buy groceries, go to clinics, or meet other crucial needs. By orienting development and amenities around transit, governments can create the conditions for more sustainable development.

Priorities of Auto-Free Design

Auto Free Design prioritizes sustainable transport over non-sustainable transport. Infrastructure is set up to make walking, bicycling, and using transit faster, cheaper, and easier than driving. The design of the system prevents unnecessary car use. These designs integrate principles that counter unjust social, economic, and transportation policies that require auto use to meet needs. People should not be forced to own an automobile to get to work, go to school, or get healthcare.

Benefits of Sustainable Transport

What would happen if urban areas were set up so that people who walk, bicycle, and use transit would take priority over people who drive their automobiles? Auto-related injuries and deaths may be reduced. As fewer cars pollute the air, land, water, people, plants, and animals, environmental damage may fall. As people walk, bicycle, and use transit, they exercise more, and this can make people healthier, which may reduce the required health care. While this may not benefit hospitals in a market system, people and society may benefit. Infrastructure would be set up to give transport advantages to people who walk, bicycle, or use transit. Many positive consequences could be generated, but some drivers will lose some of the convenience and function of an automobile.

Auto-Free Design to Sustain Transport

Auto Free Design prioritizes transportation and development in ways that allow people to live without destroying our means to live. Within an auto-free system, auto-use is the slowest, most expensive, and most dangerous way to move. Walking, bicycling, and using transit are the fastest, cleanest, safest, and most sustainable ways to transport people and objects. Incentives within the system encourage people to walk, ride bicycles, and use transit. Imagine what would happen if a city provided huge and beautiful walkways, bike lanes, and transit while letting unnecessary, inefficient, and dangerous vehicle infrastructure fade away. We want to provide ways for people to live a healthy lifestyle while reducing our global warming and ecological footprint.

Sustainable Transport Reduces Health Care Costs

Transportation, development, and health care are related, integrated, and necessary parts of a system of meeting needs. Imagine how much less health care we would need if we cut automobile accidents in half if people began to walk twice as much as they do now or if we set up our living systems to allow people to walk to meet needs. If the impact of the transportation system on the health care system is not considered, we will not be able to address the central problem the system is generating. Does our system encourage injuries and death with a market-based system? If hospitals were paid based on the number of people they kept healthy, would they be lobbying for less auto traffic and more people walking, bicycling, and using transit?

Transition to Sustainable

Another transport system, which grows out of the existing transit network, generates solutions that address global warming, transport safety, and the health of people, plants, and animals. As development is centered around transit, auto-oriented transport will fade. Streets will turn into walkways, bike lanes, and transit. As pavement is reduced, more land may be available for housing, gardens, and parks. Moving from an auto-oriented society toward transit infrastructure is a way to reduce fossil fuel use and make urban areas more sustainable.

Transition to Sustainable; Identify the Problem

If we don't change our priorities to adapt to new conditions, we will not have priorities. We can avoid crisis management by making changes to the current system before it crashes. A long-term plan can make the transition from auto-oriented living to auto-free living. As a nation, we will be healthier if people use their power to move instead of moving vehicles to move people. Let's focus on moving goods and people more than focusing on moving automobiles. This moves from a philosophy of dependence to one of proactive, steady growth that maximizes options with the most benefits.

Transition to Sustainable; Priorities of a Sustainable Transport System

The priorities of a sustainable transportation system create economic incentives for people to walk, ride bicycles, and use transit. If people can access a grocery store, laundromat, library, and clinic within a fifteen-minute walk, they won't have to drive. People are likelier to use it if it's a safe and pleasant walk outside the context of fast and loud traffic. The priority of a sustainable transport system is to make infrastructure that allows people to walk, bicycle, or use transit to move.

Market Incentives For Sustainable Transport Pollution Tax

Governments can quickly change from fossil fuel vehicles to electric vehicles by increasing the cost of fossil fuel transport and reducing the cost of non-fossil fuel transport. Increasing the cost of buying, using, and disposing of a car can encourage drivers to use other options. Car use requires vast outlays for public infrastructure, police, and regulatory agencies. Governments can make more sustainable transport by using market-based incentives to reduce auto use, which consumes large amounts of public resources.

Market Incentive for Sustainable Transport;

Fossil Fuel Reduction Incentives

If governments make fossil fuels the most expensive option, people will choose another way. Taxing fossil fuel use and using that money for sustainable transport is a smart option. Subsidizing the cost of electric vehicles with batteries charged by the sun, wind, or other renewable energy is a project to fund.

Sustainable Transport and Development

Sustainable transport is impossible without sustainable development. One should feed and complement the other. Cities can build a framework for development around a transit system. Development should include shops, clinics, housing, and jobs within a short walk from transit. Transit can frame development. As transit expands, development can fill in undeveloped areas. Overbuilt suburbs may improve by putting in a transit stop. Rapid transit, either bus or subway, should serve high-density regions. Quality transit may lead to quality development. This is a common way to add urban density to an area.

Transition to Sustainable: Liberation from Codes of Domination

Transitioning from auto use to auto-free transport may require a consensus among transport users and leadership from the main sectors of society, including businesses, governments, non-profit groups, and individuals. Governments can change a city's infrastructure from an auto-oriented transport and development system to a system in which people can easily walk, bicycle, or ride transit to live. The more a city makes those changes, the more it may serve the needs of the people of the city. As cities begin to realize they are competing against other cities around the world for business contracts, it will become apparent that cities must reduce the cost of transport, healthcare, housing, and food to compete with other cities worldwide. Sustainable infrastructure sets up the conditions for people to live well without using an automobile.

Long Range Planning

Cities develop long-term regional transport and development plans but may encounter obstacles as administrations change priorities. Gaining broad support pays off in the long run. Seek to address all objections as soon as possible. The 20-50-year plan outlines goals and processes to govern transport and development appropriately. Long-term plans allow governments to change incrementally, which may bring the least strain to those with the most to gain. In general, cities are interested in providing the means to meet needs efficiently, appropriately, and sustainably. Auto-free design is a tool for cities to use to move toward an integrated, long-term, sustainable transport and development plan that unites the interests of public and private entities toward sustainable living.

Adaptation in the Transport System

Cities make transport more efficient by using transit to move large numbers of people between destinations. These economies of scale improve efficiency, conserve resources, provide faster service, and minimize environmental damage. Pollution may be reduced by maximizing non-motorized transport. As infrastructure for walking and bicycling increases, the means for people to move while polluting less becomes possible. Integrating pleasant walk and bikeways into transit connections can increase transit use. Minimizing pollution requires efficient transportation that serves appropriate development. Large numbers of single-occupancy vehicles and private automobiles are unacceptable in dense cities.

Transport System Resource Conservation and Efficiency

Conserving resources is one way to increase the efficiency of the transport system. Walking, bicycling, and riding transit require less energy than driving a car. Further benefits accrue as people exercise more and visit clinics and hospitals less. Hospitals reduce energy use as they serve fewer patients. Cities minimize energy use by reducing vehicle infrastructure while increasing walking, bicycling, and transit infrastructure. People reduce energy use when walking, cycling, or taking transit instead of driving. Businesses reduce transport costs by subsidizing walking, bicycling, or transit use. Media reduce transport costs when they educate the public about the benefits of sustainable transport.

Non-motorized Transport

Non-motorized transport infrastructure, which includes walkways and bikeways, can feed a rapid transit system in pleasant and efficient ways. Safe and enjoyable non-motorized routes may increase transit use. Non-motorized transit infrastructure should be lit at night, surrounded by shops, clinics, recreation, and work destinations, and provide a space for art and permaculture.

Evaluating Transport Systems

One measure of development is to what extent it meets needs within walking distance. One option is to orient shops, clinics, stores, workplaces, and housing within a five or ten-minute walk from where people live. For further destinations, transit provides a safe, healthy means to move without an automobile. Transit complements communities that meet needs locally.

Using Public Transport for Parcels

Trains and buses can be designed to haul large parcels. Doing so would expand the function of transit to include moving objects. Trains can limit the size of packages to what can be loaded and unloaded quickly. Carrying cargo would be suitable for businesses located near transit stops. Businesses could package cargo to fit on trains and buses. Buses and trains could be designed to haul standard-size packages of larger sizes and weights than people can carry. Local cargo buses, cars, subways, and trains could be integrated into a national network to move freight efficiently. Packages could be set up so the passenger trains carry packages when they aren't full. These cargo trains and buses could feed coops, non-profits, and businesses, especially during non-peak hours. All of this depends on the design and engineering of cargo that can be moved on and off easily and quickly and on people who are educated and trained to use it efficiently.

Regional Integration

Integrating towns and suburbs surrounding a city with transit is a goal of a regional transport system. Building transit stops in outlying urban areas is a way to organize development around transit and minimize costly, inefficient vehicle infrastructure. Often, development expands without integrating transit. If transit is faster than auto use, people will be more likely to use it. If walk and bikeways are lined with shops, clinics, recreation destinations, and workplaces, people will be more likely to use them. Development can be located near transit stops or along the non-motorized transport lanes. With time, low-density development can increase to higher densities.

Self-Reliance in an Auto-Free System

Within auto free design, opportunities exist for people to develop more self-reliant ways to live. When people don't own a vehicle, they require less money to live, and for most, this means more time to do other things. If pavement is reduced or eliminated, more land is available for permaculture and planting gardens. If the land, air, and water aren't polluted, people can use the fruits of the land for healing or sustenance. Self-reliance can buffer people from the extremes of capitalism. If people can meet their needs in the community or through their skills, they have less need for corporations, jobs, and the state. Auto-free design is compatible with a non-fascist way of life that allows more freedom to live without so much time spent making money.

As globalization increases competition for the lowest-paid workers, cities must find ways to reduce living expenses so that workers can live well on less money. From another angle, cities that don't minimize their transport costs per person may have a less competitive edge than cities that minimize their transport costs. Minimizing transport costs with an auto-free design strategy can reduce health care costs while providing a higher quality of life as pollution is reduced and more space is available for plants, animals, and people.

Goals of Auto-Free Design

One measure of a transport system is safety. safety is the most critical measure of transportation. The rate of profit is not more important than safety, convenience, and comfort, function, or the ability to make life easier are not more important than safety. Somehow, safety got lost in the commercials, in the flash of chrome, in the shadows of those who already have too much. Still, governments and corporations claim that they are making driving safer, but how much does this matter if over 40,000 people die each year from driving automobiles and another 64,000 from air pollution? Auto Free Design puts the safety and health of people before profits or automobiles.

For some, this idea makes no sense, and to people who know of no other alternative, it may be difficult to imagine anything else. If you've never owned a car and have used transit, you won't know what it means to own a car. Until people have a fair choice to use both, cities may lose the opportunity to reduce auto use.

Reducing Auto Use Generates Many Benefits

Reducing auto use is a goal of Auto Free Design. Less auto use may reduce death and injury from vehicle crashes and pollution. This reduces pain and suffering and the cost of driving. Cities that maximize walking, bicycling, and using transit can reduce infrastructure for vehicles. Since vehicle use requires a large police force and judicial system to control drivers, the city can save vast amounts of money by reducing auto use. As people walk and bicycle, they exercise more than if they use a vehicle, reducing health care costs. Providing safe, healthy, efficient, affordable, and sustainable transport options for people are the goals of Auto Free Design.

Sustainable Transport Infrastructure

Sustainable transport infrastructure, which allows people to meet needs within walking distance, is more sustainable than auto-oriented infrastructure. Providing the infrastructure for people to live without an automobile is a goal of Auto Free Design. A person should be able to walk to work, buy groceries, shop for clothes, and visit a clinic or hospital within a twenty-minute walk or a short transit ride. Putting people first is a relevant, appropriate, and necessary criterion for evaluating design and development. Auto Free Design empowers people to live outside the oppressive conditions of auto-oriented development.

Transport infrastructure, built with materials and methods that minimize environmental damage, is more sustainable than materials and methods that don't reduce fossil fuel use. Roads with concrete and asphalt require large amounts of fossil fuels. Transport infrastructure can become more sustainable if governments require materials and methods that minimize fossil fuel use.

Rewarding Sweat Equity and Healthy Living

Auto-free design replaces the logic of an auto-oriented transport system with a logic that prioritizes person-powered transport. Within this system, the priority in terms of money, infrastructure, and design is to facilitate the power of people to move while integrating into a transit system. Within a car-free system, the goal is to create infrastructure for walking and bicycling. So the easiest route to a store, school, clinic, or workplace is not driving a car but walking, riding a bicycle, or using transit. In areas where this is the case, people enjoy the benefits of an urban area free of cars.

Cities of the Future Go Strong and Green

Cities that move away from the auto-oriented model will thrive while others stagnate from the fossil fuel transport infrastructure burden. The car system kills and injures too many people, pollutes too much air, land, and water, and reduces economic efficiency. It's a mega-tax on people and a way to limit the power of people to be free of oppressive codes. Transport codes that require auto use make people work more to get money to pay for vehicle use. For many, this is more challenging than walking, bicycling, or using transit. To be strong and mighty, cities can use local materials and methods for transport infrastructure and make cities where people don't need a car to live well.

Cities of the Future Implement Sustainable Transport Plans

Auto-free design creates a healthier transport system for people, animals, plants and the environment. The current system can be improved to minimize conflicts between pedestrians, bicyclists, and vehicle users. The more we isolate vehicles from pedestrians, bicycle riders, and transit users, the safer people will be. If we set up an infrastructure so that the safest, fastest, most pleasant route is walking or cycling, people will use those transport methods. Cities and nations that make this transition will have more economic advantages than cities that don't make that transition. We can improve people's health by enhancing the air quality that people breathe. If we reduce pavement by 1% per year for fifty years and replace that pavement with green space, we can create a healthier urban environment for people, plants, and animals.

Chapter 6
AFD Examples

Transition to Auto Free

Urban areas with less car use are scattered around the planet. In these areas, infrastructure for walking, bicycling, and using transit is expanded while vehicle infrastructure is reduced. Over the last 20 years, New York City has increased bike lanes and pedestrian areas and reduced vehicle pavement. This is a gradual, step-by-step approach to facilitate walking, bicycling, and using transit. This method is standard in forward-leaning urban areas. In Europe, city centers with less auto use are common. In China, new cities are constructed to maximize non-motorized transit and minimize auto use.

Changing the Economic Conditions

Using Government Action to Reduce Traffic

The price of transport influences the choices people make. In some areas, walking and bicycling are the least expensive, most pleasant ways to move. In other areas, the only choice people have is to use a vehicle because the distance between destinations is too far to walk, bicycle, or use transit. Governments can increase the cost of driving, which may encourage people to use alternatives.

Methods of reducing traffic include:

• Reduce the cost of sustainable transport while increasing the cost of vehicle use.

• Make walking, bicycling, and transit use cheaper, more pleasant, and more efficient.

• Increasing fossil fuel prices and vehicle taxes.

• Increase gas tax to fund walkways, bike lanes, and transit.

• Subsidize walking, bicycling, and transit use.

• Implement a carbon tax on high-emission vehicles.

• Increase taxes on sprawling development.

• Subsidize transit-oriented development.

• Tax fossil fuel transport items that are difficult to renew, reuse, or recycle.

• Increase fees on parking and single occupancy vehicles.

• Subsidize electric vehicles with non-recurring fees for fossil fuel vehicles.

• Develop transit to rural areas, including walkways, bike lanes, and transit.

• Subsidize sustainable transport and development in rural areas.

Using Market Forces to Reduce Traffic

Governments can reduce traffic by increasing the cost of driving. Taxes on gas, vehicles, roads, tunnels, and congested areas can encourage sustainable transport use. As governments increase the cost of buying, using, and disposing of a vehicle, many benefits will accrue. Electronic vehicle metering devices can direct traffic to less congested areas by charging tolls based on the number of people using the system.

Increase Infrastructure for Walking, Bicycling, and Using Transit

In areas dominated by vehicle infrastructure, converting to non-motorized transport may require clever thinking, long-term planning, and a will to succeed. Changing infrastructure is a colossal project, especially if water, sewer, and electrical lines are in the street. Long-term development plans should expand walking, bicycle, and transit infrastructure. Development around transit instead of freeway exits may reduce traffic and increase sustainable activities. As infrastructure for sustainable methods improves, benefits will accrue, but people will still have to walk and bicycle to get the most out of the transport system. The following are examples of ways to increase infrastructure for sustainable transport.

- Make plans and goals to increase sustainable transit infrastructure.

- Make plans and goals to reduce pavement by 1% per year.

- Make safe, pleasant, and efficient walkways and bike lanes to feed transit.

- Reduce modal conflict by separating pedestrians and bicycle users from vehicles.

- Make coherent long-term plans that integrate transit throughout the region.

- Transition from auto-oriented infrastructure to transit-oriented infrastructure.

Leaders Govern Change of Mind

Leaders in alternative groups, government, education, and media can direct people to move sustainably. As people experience the consequences of global warming, they realize why we must adapt or lose our means to live. Being open to walking, bicycling, or transit can reduce fossil fuel use. What if we saw a public service announcement for sustainable transport for every car commercial? A curriculum that explains global warming and sustainable transport and development solutions should be required in all schools. In media, leaders must alert people about alternatives to driving and solutions in the public interest. Leaders who lead by example and are the change people want to see can make a difference. Implanting the seed in people's minds and leading them to discover it will make a change. Highlighting commendable projects and behavior can advance sustainable transport.

City Sponsored Competitions Can Activate the Public to Embrace Sustainable Transport

Competitions to be the city that makes the most bike trips engage citizens in a culture of sustainable transport. The Netherlands uses contests to motivate people to use bicycles. Cities compete to be "The Cycling City of Netherlands." "The Race Around the Netherlands" is a ride around the country that passes through some of the best areas of the Netherlands. The Amstel Gold Race in the province of Limburg is an annual race in the spring. These events activate groups of cyclists to make a culture of cycling that supports and advances sustainable transport and development. Many realize that walking, riding a bicycle, and using transit improves the standard of living. With the cost of driving a vehicle much higher than bicycle riding, the Netherlands can use economic incentives for people to bicycle. Less money is spent on transport, and people get more exercise as they walk and bike. This reduces health care costs. As people breathe less pollution, fewer will die from vehicle exhaust.

Changing Mindset

A common idea in the US is that using a car is better than walking, bicycling, and using transit. As a kid and throughout life, I've seen lots of car commercials. Vehicles cruise effortlessly through pristine areas with fit, trim, and wealthy people. In our family, the car was also a status symbol. Why walk? Just take the car; there is no need to add labor; let the machine do the work. Hiking, bicycling, and transit may be challenging if people always use a vehicle. The conveniences and comforts of vehicles are seductive. People may cling to old habits without government, media, and education leadership. Appropriate governments phase out auto infrastructure with bike lanes, walkways, and transit, which can change how people think and use transport.

Change of Mind Infrastructure Changes Public Opinion

If you watch car commercials, do you think you will tend to walk, bicycle, or use transit? What if you see examples of how people live well without using a vehicle? In Manhattan, 75% of the people do not own a car. With good transit, walkways, and bike lanes, the infrastructure can change minds. With too many vehicles, the rules are more complicated, and congestion makes it faster to use a bicycle. Congestion and the pain of driving change minds.

Change of Mind Connecting with Nature Can Change Public Opinion

If people only watch Dallas or Dynasty, they may assume that a posh-looking place to live with a fancy car is a success. For others, healthy people, plants, air, land, and water are a higher priority. Measuring life with money and objects can lead to an empty life. In terms of transport, if we can make something safe, affordable, appropriate and efficient using local, re-useable or sustainable resources, perhaps people will use it, however, if there's a lazier alternative like vehicle use, many may choose that. With a combination of efforts, the public mind can change.

Low-Risk Alternatives Motivate People to Use Existing Infrastructure in Sustainable Ways

People may walk and bicycle if they are motivated. Least work for most gain is a slogan in permaculture and a chant for those looking to get work done. Allocating road space for bike lanes and reducing parking may encourage bicycle use without changing infrastructure. Going for the low-hanging fruit may be a strategy that yields quick gains to add traction to a transition to sustainable transportation. If people recognize the broader arguments that support energy-efficient transport, they may embrace relevant and appropriate solutions. Education and motivation can feed the desire to walk, bicycle, or use transit. K-12 courses could educate children about the safety and benefits of walking, bicycling, and using transit. Training people once can lead to a lifetime of public benefits. Government incentives for people to live without a vehicle could reduce auto use. Reducing or not maintaining vehicle infrastructure could pressure people to use alternatives to fossil fuel vehicles.

Use Existing Infrastructure

For some, if a road, building, or infrastructure is wrong or unnecessary, the best way to deal with it is to knock it down, start over, and do it the right way with updated methods and materials. If we don't consider cost, efficiency, or environmental consequences, this may be the best option, but what if we could find a way to use what we have and make minor adjustments to our way of life? Now, that takes more effort on a personal level, but brings economic and health benefits. An active, motivated public that realizes the benefits of a low footprint may generate benefits for everyone. Also, the longer we use infrastructure to its fullest potential, the higher the return on our investment.

Conditions for Sustainable Transport: Without Sustainable Governance, the Carnage will Continue

Governments determine the future of transport. Market incentives can rapidly transform transport. Taxing fossil fuel use while subsidizing alternatives could influence people to use sustainable transport methods. Building infrastructure for safe and pleasant walkways, bike lanes, and transit can make a big difference. People can only walk or bicycle if destinations are 20 miles or more if they use transit or another method. You can only choose if the infrastructure is there. People need money to use most transport except walking and bicycling. Governments create the conditions for sustainable transport and development. Prioritizing building and operating infrastructure for people to walk, bicycle, and use transit can reduce fossil fuel use and secure the conditions for humans to live on the planet.

Appropriate Density

- Higher densities can generate more efficient use of resources and an active social culture

Density measures the number of people per square mile in urban areas. Low-density development or sprawl, common in most small and midsize American cities, requires large amounts of infrastructure per person. Higher densities in New York and Chicago, which have more buildings per square mile and larger buildings that house more people, generate more efficient use of infrastructure and more dynamic social conditions. More people use the same water, sewer, electric, and cable lines per square mile. These economies of scale can be more efficient.

In Groningen, Netherlands, They Made Bike Paths Instead of Road Ways

The difference is stunning. Most US cities are low-density and built around roads more than transit. High density is often located around transit. Sidewalks and bike lanes combine better with transit than freeway exits and parking lots. To increase density in Houston, TX, they built transit to outer areas. This creates opportunities for non-vehicle users and has a lower carbon footprint.

Arguments Against AFD Examples

People are used to driving. Many will not welcome giving up comfort and convenience for economy and environmental sustainability. Others realize and enjoy the chance to live without a vehicle. Transit adds an option that gives you time to sleep and read, look out windows, write, do art, and relax. Without proper education, media, and governance, transitioning from low to high density may require significant patience and dedication. One can design ways to avoid the car malaise by setting goals and making habits. You never know when you will be a victim.

Common Examples

Examples of auto-free Design are common if you know what to look for. Auto-free Design includes infrastructure for walking, bicycling, or using transit. Bus, subway, and train stops are examples of transit infrastructure. Development is oriented around transit stops. Ideally, sidewalks and bike lanes connect to transit in safe, pleasant, and efficient ways. If people are engaged and push for better transit, they are more likely to get it. Bike lanes are examples of sustainable transport and should be the safest, most pleasant, and efficient way to get to and from a destination. Transit systems liberate people from the indentured servitude of unaffordable transport.

The Challenge and Leap of Faith: Will People Use It

Setting up infrastructure for walking, cycling, and transit is part of the equation. Setting up the finest infrastructure for walking and bicycling is possible, but people need to use it. If no other option is available, people will use it. Selective use of auto infrastructure will generate advantages. Convenience and cost determine many transit choices. If there's a nice bike lane, will I use it if I can use my car instead? Both options add choices but may not encourage the desired result. If there is no way to use a car, then people will use sustainable methods. If sustainable methods are less costly, people with less money will use them. The luxury of modern life is to have both options. The priority for progress is to use transit to reduce inequality and ensure the viability of the planet.

Using Transit to Reduce Inequality

Transit is an opportunity. Add a bicycle to the equation, and the benefits increase. People who can't afford or don't want to use a vehicle generate advantages from transit. It means access to what vehicle owners can get without a vehicle. Many find it easier to get a job with decent transit. Transit can reduce inequality by providing the following:

- Access to housing, health care, food, and clothing without a vehicle.

- Access to work, schools, and businesses without cars.

- Access to meet needs locally without using fossil fuels.

- Access to the pleasures of life, including shops, restaurants, and entertainment.

Many who experience the good life without transit don't go back and rarely miss the experience of driving a vehicle. After all, why worry about an accident when you can use transit? For lower-income people, transit generates access to the rest of the world without the impossible burden of vehicle ownership. In Manhattan, NY, 75% of the people don't own a vehicle. Many could have a car but choose to avoid the hassles and troubles of auto ownership.

Green Challenge: Reduce Inequality and Improve Air, Land, Water, Plants, Animals, and People.

Green cities elevate the standard of living while improving habitat for plants and animals. Transit corridors integrate bike lanes, walkways, flowers, trees, rivers, lakes, and bees. Aromatic and beautiful plants enrich a neighborhood. Families and friends work the soil, harvest plants, and use mother nature against illness, loneliness, and boredom. Cities of green transform life, liberating people from the constraints of auto use.

Ideas to provide sustainable transport can be applied in different ways. Often, building something new is more accessible than fixing what you have. Cities that can use what they have can gain. Others may be forced to build from scratch. Madison, Wisconsin, has a pedestrian mall on State Street that connects the Capitol and the University, two popular destinations. The pedestrian mall allows buses, emergency vehicles, and bicycles. It's a popular place with lots of people, which is in stark contrast to the rest of the city, which, because of its low density, looks deserted most of the time.

Norway Increases Electric Vehicle Ownership with Government-Controlled Market Forces

Norway implemented market incentives to increase the number of electric vehicles and reduce fossil fuel-powered vehicles. Electric cars are exempt from the purchase tax and value-added tax. They are also exempt from ferry charges, road tolls, and tunnel-use charges. With free parking, free battery charging, and free use of bus lanes, so many people bought them that the government will increase prices. Norway has demonstrated that market forces can quickly increase electric car use.

Groningen, Netherlands: Makes Transition from Vehicle Transport to Bicycle Transport

Groningen is a city in the Netherlands that chose to rid itself of vehicle congestion by prioritizing the construction of bike lanes instead of car lanes. In the 1970s, a left-oriented government decided against building more freeways and roads. Instead of ramming a freeway through neighborhoods, they expanded bike lanes, reduced vehicle pavement, and increased auto-free areas in the city's center. Groningen is a model for many cities looking to use bicycles to free themselves from the auto plague. Nearly 2 out of 3 trips are made with bicycles, which is more than most European cities.

Ho Chi Minh City Bus Rapid Transit Changes Minds About Transit

Ho Chi Minh City is building a region-wide Bus Rapid Transit (BRT) system. BRT provides dedicated bus lanes and fast boarding to move people with less infrastructure costs than subways. Designing a pleasant, efficient transport system to replace and augment the dangerous, overused roadways is a way to change minds about transit. People may choose transit over vehicle use as they see, experience, and use pleasant transit.

Arcosanti

Arcosanti is a small village project located in the desert, 70 miles north of Phoenix, Arizona. It covers an area of 25 acres and has 50-150 residents who live and work there. Started in 1970, the completed project will include 5,000 people. The project is an example of a small town with minimal vehicle use. Villagers make art and live without needing a vehicle, increasing the time people have to live, work, and make art.

Stuyvesant Town-Peter Cooper Village

Imagine living in a park in the middle of New York City. Stuyvesant Town-Peter Cooper Village is a private residential development on the East Side of Lower Manhattan that covers 80 acres and houses 25,000 people in 89 buildings 6-10 stories tall. With ample green space, trees, a playground, and indoor community areas, the development allows a pleasant respite from the traffic and congestion surrounding it. The project, designed and built from 1940-1946, was set up to increase the supply and quality of housing in the area for white people. Six hundred buildings were demolished, and 11,000 people were forced out. The project has a few roadways for deliveries and emergencies but very little traffic. Like most housing in NYC, most of this housing is not affordable.

Eco-cities

Sustainable transport provides the infrastructure to make walking, cycling, and using transit easy. Eco-cities are evaluated according to the following criteria:

- Can people walk, bicycle, or use transit to meet their needs?
- Does it use a sustainable amount of fossil fuels?
- Was it built sustainably?
- How does it improve the quality of land, air, and water?
- Does it minimize and make waste harmless?
- Was it built on land not useable for farming and other more appropriate functions?
- Is there easy access to safe and pleasant gardens, parks, and wild areas?
- What percent of trips are made sustainably (walk, bicycle, transit)?
- Is housing affordable?
- Does it provide infrastructure for sports and recreation?

Build it New

China is rapidly urbanizing. Peasants are moving from the country to the city. With large amounts of pollution and the need for more urban infrastructure, China is in an excellent position to develop Eco City infrastructure. What is Eco City infrastructure?

- 90% of travel is done by walking, bicycling or using transit.
- Buildings and vehicles use the least energy and raw materials to support life.

- Compact Design minimizes transport and maximizes efficient use of infrastructure.

Chinese Example Urbanization and Extreme Pollution Motivate Chinese to Lead the World in the Design and Building of Eco-Cities.

The Chinese government is building 285 eco-cities that minimize energy use and pollution. The surge in building cities started after the revolution in 1949. The goal is to provide practical urban environments that harmonize humans, nature, and the built environment to use fewer resources, reduce carbon emissions, recycle more, and use clean fuels like solar and wind power. Cities will be less industrial, more pleasant, and more green. So what does this have to do with Auto Free Design? Most cities are built with the assumption that the dominant mode of transport is with a vehicle; here, more emphasis is put on designs that minimize auto use and use the least energy to move people and goods. These cities could radically change how people build and use cities. The assumption is that transportation is oriented around streets with vehicles; a city without those assumptions could look, feel, and operate quite differently. Imagine not thinking about getting hit by a car while crossing the street.

Tianjin Eco-City Demonstration Project

The Tianjin Eco-City project is a collaboration between China and Singapore to develop and build a replicable, scalable Eco-City. Variations of this model could be applied to different urban challenges. The goal is to make an environmentally friendly, economically viable, and energy-efficient environment. Creating social, economic, and environmental harmony is one approach. Technology adapted must be practical, affordable, and commercially feasible so that it can be used in other cities and scalable so that it can be made in larger quantities without setting up another system. Imagine transit stops fed with walkways and bike lanes in a dense urban area.

EcoCity Infrastructure

EcoCities set up infrastructure for people to live sustainably using the least resources and making infrastructure to make walking, bicycling, and transit the safest, most efficient, most pleasant, and most economical way to move between destinations. Building roads, streets, and parking is the opposite of what an Eco City does. Sustainable transport is one part of an Eco City. The other is sustainable development. Sustainable development makes infrastructure that uses the least fossil fuels to house people, governments, and businesses. High-performance buildings minimize energy use. Buildings are made airtight, with insulated walls, windows, doors, and ceilings, and powered without using fossil fuels. Sustainable transport works best with Sustainable development, which allows people to live well without using a vehicle.

Setting up cities for people to walk, bicycle, and use transit can be done with existing technology. With many examples from around the world, thoughtful design in the public interest can liberate people from the scourge of auto-oriented transport. Electric vehicles will solve some of the problems of an auto-oriented transport system, but the central system of roads may still exist. If governments expand sustainable transport infrastructure while reducing fossil fuel vehicle infrastructure, people will accrue many benefits.

Chapter 7
AFD Global Warming Solutions for Transport

Nations will Stand or Fall Based on Their Ability to Prepare for and Adapt to Climate Change

The Situation

The transport system in the US was set up when the assumptions for fossil fuel use included the following.

- Fossil fuel pollution is not a problem.

- There is an infinite supply of cheap fossil fuels.

After a couple hundred years of limitless fossil fuel use, it becomes apparent that using fossil fuel to power our vehicles and buildings will accelerate global warming, destroying the conditions in which people live. So now we live with infrastructure for transport and housing that needs to be updated. The cars, buildings, and infrastructure require too much fossil fuel. So now we must adapt or face endless catastrophes as global warming expands and intensifies.

Changing Mindset: Can it Be Done Before It's Too Late?

The solutions are obvious and many, but humans develop habits that take work to change. Some people live in safe zones where global warming has brought minimal inconvenience and few negative impacts. Other people have lived through hurricanes, extreme heat waves, fires, and floods. For some, it's evident that the fossil fuel economy is leading us to disaster. For many humans, the evidence isn't conclusive unless they feel the pain,

Changing Leadership: Can it be done before it's too late?

As of 2018, a consensus among leaders is apparent except for a few corrupt and rogue states, including the US. Many leaders inside and outside of government have accepted our situation and are moving quickly to reduce or eliminate fossil fuel use, both in transport and buildings. We may be just a few disasters, or payoffs to the corruption machine to transform energy use and production to eliminate or vastly reduce fossil fuel use.

Electric Cars

Electric vehicles will quickly replace fossil fuel vehicles in progressive countries that acknowledge the problem and make solutions. However, what about other countries where a vast infrastructure and money-making machine make the transition more problematic? The transition could be made quickly in the United States. Already, other countries have working models. People will buy electric vehicles if they are cheaper and better than fossil fuel vehicles. Norway has proven this already. They quickly increased the number of electric cars by 30% by reducing the cost of owning and operating an electric vehicle while keeping the cost of fossil fuel vehicles high.

Self-Driving Electric Cars

The future of transport is in motion. Self-driving cars, which may be safer than human-driven cars, make driving safer and reduce the cost of transportation for the government. Nearly all accidents, 95% or more, are caused by human error. Self-driving cars make fewer mistakes and have proven to be safer. If self-driving electric cars reduce accidents to a small fraction of what they are today, the next problem may be to prevent endless congestion. Systems that charge higher fees for congested areas may reduce this problem.

Solar and Wind Farms, and Batteries and Clean Energy Can Transform the Energy Equation

Solar and wind farms and large batteries transform the energy equation. As these technologies produce more power, less fossil fuel power will be needed. These are off-the-shelf technologies; most of the engineering and production methods have been tested, and now it's more a matter of fine-tuning. Yes, quantum changes may happen, but these technologies have been in place for a while and have stood the test; the question becomes whether or not this will lead to significant reductions in fossil fuel production and use.

Making Global Warming-Proof Transport Infrastructure

Floods, storm surges, and hurricanes damage and destroy roads, bridges, and tunnels. One solution is to provide floodwater another place to go while increasing porous surfaces that allow water to drain into the soil. Even if this reduced floodwater level, in some areas, it may be impossible or so easy to move highways or control the forces of hurricanes to overtake transport infrastructure. It may be possible to strengthen and bolster infrastructure to minimize damage in these areas. Some designs may use giant solar and wind arrays that generate electricity and slow down the force of a massive storm.

Infrastructure Required to Escape Extreme Weather Events May Be Destroyed During Extreme Weather

Extreme weather, including fires, flooding, tornados, and hurricanes, can destroy roads used to travel out of severe weather. Downed trees, power lines, and buildings may prevent people from leaving an extreme weather event. Governments can evacuate populations before some extreme events like hurricanes. Some storms can't be predicted. Governments must take measures to prepare for severe weather.

Rebuilding Infrastructure May Be Impossible for a Long Time After an Extreme Weather Event

Massive storms can wipe out power, pavement, and transport infrastructure for miles. When a low-lying road is washed out, an alternative route may increase the distance to destinations. Alternate routes will be jammed up, and transport will be slow. Supplies, materials, equipment, and tools may be difficult or impossible to get after an extreme weather event. Labor will be in short supply. Progress will go slow. Shortages may be expected. People will have to adapt and may make things work. This can make roads more dangerous if shortcuts are taken. It's much easier to fortify infrastructure before extreme weather than after storms destroy the means to fix anything.

Walking and Bicycling Infrastructure May be More Resilient Than Other Infrastructure

Sidewalks and bikeways are less work to set up and maintain than infrastructure for automobiles and transit. If people can meet their needs within walking distance, they may be more able to keep going after a catastrophic event. People can walk or bicycle a short ride in a well-designed area to meet needs. If required infrastructure is kept to a minimum, less will be destroyed in an extreme weather event. Systems that allow people to live with the most minor infrastructure may provide significant advantages in the age of global warming.

Build up Transport Infrastructure to Withstand Extreme Weather Events

Infrastructure has different vulnerable areas. Subways don't do well in flooding. Bridges may succumb to high winds, while a subway may not be affected. Roads may survive high winds but wash away from storm surges. Designs respond to design specifications. Preparing exit routes from large urban areas is a priority. Other routes that are the only means to leave may become impossibly congested in or after an emergency.

- Infrastructure must be built to higher standards.

- Infrastructure must be built to withstand extreme weather events, including fires, flooding, tornadoes, and hurricanes

Preparing Transport Infrastructure for Extreme Weather Can Save Lives and Reduce or Eliminate Property Damage

Reinforcing existing infrastructure requires much less time, energy, and money than rebuilding after a catastrophe. Preparing for extreme weather events may not be easy. Governments may know the most significant threats and must carefully target their spending. If it's a coastal city with a history of floods, preparing for heat waves may not make sense. Sometimes, there will be multiple threats. The Midwest gets tornados and heat waves. Projects must be carefully worked out to use infrastructure money strategically to prepare for the most likely extreme weather event.

In some cases, an evacuation plan is needed. This plan may require upgraded roads to withstand flooding or other weather-related events. Cities will need to be more agile, adaptive, and strategic. A well-functioning transport infrastructure can prevent millions from death and injury.

Preparing Pavement to Reduce Extreme Heat and Flooding Impacts

- Plant more trees to reduce the heat of pavement.

- Use permeable pavement to reduce flooding and pollution.

- Reduce pavement to reduce heat-absorbing materials.

- Paint asphalt a light color, like white, to reflect heat.

- Bury electric power cables so lines don't blow down and prevent transport.

Prepare Bridges to Withstand More Extreme Heat and Wind

- Test bridges before extreme weather to identify weak areas to improve.

- Specify materials and methods that withstand higher wind speeds and temperatures.

- Reinforce bridges and infrastructure to withstand extreme heat and force.

- Fortifying bridges before extreme weather can prevent more significant problems.

Prepare Tunnels to Withstand Flooding

- Tunnels may be sealed off to prevent flood waters from entering.

- Tunnels should have drains to empty flood waters.

- Drains should go into large open areas below sea level.

- Make drains to low-lying wetlands to absorb floodwaters.

Prepare Airports for Flooding

Low-lying airports flood after significant rainfalls, storm surges, and hurricanes. Airports may have to be moved or flood walls made to prevent water from entering and water diverted to lower areas.

Airports are difficult to locate, vast in scale, and present significant challenges to governments. Global warming may make low-lying airports impossible to use.

Global warming is a severe threat to transport infrastructure. Flooding, storm surges, heat waves, and hurricanes can seriously damage roads, bridges, and tunnels. Weak or damaged infrastructure is more likely to give way in extreme weather. Escape routes in weather emergencies can be built up to perform under higher stresses. Planning and retrofitting existing infrastructure can prevent death and injury and reduce infrastructure damage. Governments that prepare for disasters may be better positioned to respond later.

Chapter 8
Auto Free Cities

"Auto-free cities exist in language, definition, memory, history, imagination, and the reality people create."

Cities of the future design transport systems to maximize safe, pleasant, and affordable infrastructure that minimizes fossil fuel use and resists the extremes of Global Warming.

Cities of the future make plans that move people and goods in safe, pleasant, sustainable, and efficient ways. Locating development around transit can provide the means for people to meet needs locally. If cities can reduce auto use while increasing the number of people who walk, bicycle, and use transit, people will benefit in many ways. Auto-free planning integrates into the existing framework of transport and development. Cities that create Auto Free Zones (AFZ) will increase freedom as people choose to live in areas without the dangers, pollution, and economic limitations of auto use.

The Process

Designing cities to facilitate walking, bicycling, and transit is a step toward an Auto Free City (AFC). Changing roads, buildings, transit, and utilities often require time, money, and resources. Hence, creating long-term plans that allow significant changes to be implemented in the smallest, least painful steps makes sense. Auto-free cities begin by setting up and expanding existing auto-free areas until more extensive urban areas are set up for people to live without automobiles. Processes and plans that spring out of the enthusiasm of local people combined within a holistic framework governed by the city, state, and nation may provide lasting benefits.

Move People, not Cars.

People who walk, bicycle, use transit to get to work or school, or recreate integrate exercise into their daily routines. This exercise improves health. If fewer people use vehicles, congestion, pollution, resource use, and stress may be reduced. When enough people stop using vehicles, the city can reduce pavement. As the amount of pavement shrinks, land can be converted from auto use to other uses, including meeting needs locally, making pleasant public space, or making auto-free zones. If people walk, bicycle, and use transit instead of a car, positive benefits accrue for the individual, neighborhood, city, state, and nation.

Goals of Auto-Free Cities

Sustainable cities establish auto-free zones around transit stops, university areas, city centers, and water. Development is organized so that people can walk to meet their needs. Auto-free zones include transit, emergency, delivery, utility, and construction vehicle lanes. Car coops and parking lots can be situated outside of an auto-free area. Walkways and bike lanes should be the most direct, pleasant, and easiest way to get to popular destinations and transit. Infrastructure should minimize contact between pedestrians, bicyclers, transit users and vehicles. One of the main goals of AFD is to reduce death and injury from vehicle accidents. The less contact between non-motorized and motorized transportation, the safer the system will be. As AFZs become established, the city can expand AFZ until it becomes an auto-free city.

AUTO FREE ZONING

The city can create another class of zoning or public regulation of land. These areas, Auto Free Zones (AFZ), would not allow auto use but would allow transit, emergency, and delivery vehicles. Within an Auto Free Zone, the priorities for transportation and development focus on people and infrastructure more than automobiles. Walkways, bike lanes, and transit would be the primary forms of transport in and out of an Auto Free Zone. Auto Free Zones allow people to live in more comfort and safety as they no longer have to deal with the negative consequences of auto use. Youth, older people, and people with disabilities, those who are most vulnerable to traffic, have fewer worries, while parents wouldn't have to think about their children getting run over by cars.

Auto Free Infrastructure

Providing infrastructure, which includes streets and buildings, that allows people to meet needs within walking distance or a short transit ride will make the city more sustainable. To do this, cities coordinate transport and development in ways that maximize the benefits of walking, bicycling, and using transit while increasing the cost of driving. The more the city can make transit the fastest, cheapest, easiest, and most sustainable way to get between two points, the more it will create a safe, healthy, and competitive city in the world and the future. The city will become safer, pleasant, and livable if development plans locate businesses, clinics, and nonprofits near mass transit and within Auto Free Zones.

Bus Rapid Transit

A frame for sustainable transportation is transit, which includes subways, light rail, or Bus Rapid Transit (BRT). BRT combines the advantages of rapid loading and unrestricted lanes to make a more affordable and flexible transit system. Preloading fare collection, signal priority at intersections, and vehicle information displays can make BRT compete with auto use. BRT systems work best if they occupy lanes completely separated from other traffic. Cities may build over and underpasses through high-traffic intersections and use signal priority at less active intersections. Since BRT systems cost less and may pay for themselves, getting public support to fund the project is easier than subways and light rail. Ideally, BRT is integrated into walkways, bike lanes, and transit systems to make smooth connections and rapid access to destinations. Some examples of BRT are in Curitiba, Brazil, and Bogota, Columbia, where politicians took a significant risk to fund transit, which frees people from the constraints of automobiles.

Walk Ways and Bike Lanes

Walkways and bike lanes should be the safest, fastest, cheapest, and most pleasant way to get to transit, shops, and workplaces. At best, walkways and bike lanes are entirely separate from motorized transport to minimize death and injury from vehicles. Transportation infrastructure that requires personal power increases exercise, reducing the need for healthcare and saving people and cities a lot of money. Walkways and bike lanes combine well with sculpture, historical markers, distinctive street furniture, plants, and animals. Imagine walking through different permaculture, art, and historic zones of the city. Each cultivates a distinct presence from the neighborhood's people, plants, and animals. These connect to transit nodes, which could lead to anywhere else. Imagine walking through canopies of trees and vines without parking lots, cars, and traffic. The difference is the difference between life and death. One is alive, and the other is dead.

Benefits of Living Without Automobiles

For the city, businesses, and the public, benefits include:

- Less dangers for pedestrians, bicyclers, and transit users.

- Less pollution, noise and traffic, cleaner air, land, water, plants and animals

- Less pavements and more space for plants, animals, and people.

Rickshaws could replace taxis, people who use the gym could do the heavy lifting, and a dog could pull a sled with wheels. Unfortunately, the convenience of the automobile has trumped the creative use of personal power. As auto use is reduced, the city will come alive as people use their bodies, carts, and objects to move themselves.

City Incentives for Auto-Free Zones

Auto Free Zones can help the city to:

- Reduce death and injury from accidents and pollution.

- Reduce pain and suffering from auto use.

- Reduce victims of the transport system.

- Reduce the cost of transport.

- Reduce police and courts for traffic violations.

- Reduce emissions that cause Global Warming.

- Reduce the cost of designing, building, maintaining, and regulating roads.

- Reduce infrastructure and maintenance costs.

- Reduce traffic control costs for police and courts.

- Improve the quality of air, land, and water.

- Improve the health of people, plants and animals

- Improve the ecosystem by reducing pollution to air, land, and water

Cities can make huge gains by reducing auto use and building a sustainable transport infrastructure. Designing, building, maintaining, and controlling traffic is a significant tax on people, especially when all related costs are calculated. Losing someone in a car crash can spell economic collapse for a household. People can't operate vehicles safely. Why spend so much time moving a vehicle when people can move themselves and objects?

Automated Transport

Computers may be programmed to operate vehicles in a safer way than humans. Self-driving, electric cars are the future of transport. If safety issues were addressed, would auto-free areas make sense? Cities would still have to build infrastructure and control automated vehicles. The workload and expense may be similar to human-driven vehicles. Self-driving cars must operate at a much higher level. They must be frequently checked to maintain high-performance standards. Perhaps if robots were doing this, it could work. Vehicles would have to live up to the same standards as airplanes. We don't tolerate airplane crashes; why should we tolerate car crashes? Self-driving electric vehicles could address some safety problems with vehicles but will generate other issues, which could minimize the positive impact. If cars are safer and cheaper to run, more people will drive. Infrastructure and control would still have to be funded. These cars may be more challenging to maintain because they have many more controls. The quality of the vehicle will have to be high to operate at a much safer level. Automated transport may be safer and more efficient but requires extensive infrastructure.

Business Incentives for Auto-Free Zones

Businesses can gain by supporting sustainable transport and development. Cities require brilliant designs that produce jobs and increase their economic viability. Making low-carbon roads and buildings can boost the economy and make world leaders of those who design, build, and distribute solutions to make low-carbon transport and development infrastructure. Even though parking may be eliminated around businesses, sales increase as more people want to shop in pleasant surroundings. Converting infrastructure from an auto-oriented transportation system to auto-free transportation increases demand for construction and development projects. More bike shops, pedicabs, and auto-free services will be needed as neighborhoods, cities, and regions transition to a more sustainable region.

Neighborhood Incentives for Auto-Free Zones

Local areas with significant traffic gain the most if traffic is reduced or eliminated. Traffic is unsafe, generates air pollution and noise, and uses large amounts of land. Areas without traffic are safer, especially for children and the disadvantaged. The neighborhood becomes more pleasant with less air pollution, noise, and dust. Parents with children can rest easier if their children can play outside without the risk of a car running them over. Since walking and bicycling will become more common, people who exercise will be more likely to express the happiness coming from inside their bodies. The neighborhood will be safer, healthier, and more pleasant with less pavement, pollution, and stress from auto use.

Conversion Land Free the Land

Since parking and traffic lanes would be reduced, land may be available for non-transport uses. Communities, stakeholders, and the city could choose to convert land used for automobiles to other functions. Traffic lanes and parking lots could be transformed into gardens, shops, clinics, recycling centers, schools, or nonprofit community-oriented functions. If there's no clinic, hardware store, grocery store, or desired restaurant, one could be located on land used for parking or traffic. This land could be used to meet needs that aren't being met. With a community decision-making process, the function could integrate into the neighborhood.

Transport within AFZ

People who live within an AFZ need emergency, delivery, construction, and maintenance services. Infrastructure accommodates utility and emergency vehicles as custom allows. Police, fire, ambulance, and transit vehicles should always have access. Delivery, utility, construction, and maintenance vehicles could be more restricted.

People who live in an auto-free area can walk, bicycle, or ride transit to parking on the edge of an AFZ. One option is to locate parking lots and car coops just outside of an Auto Free Zone. For people who can't or don't want to walk, frequent transit could take people from an auto-free zone to where they want to go. Pedi-cabs and rickshaws could transport people and goods inside and outside an Auto Free Zone.

Efficient Transport

With creativity and ingenuity, people can move goods with work bikes, trailers, hand trucks, carts, dollies, and other intelligent inventions. It's a good challenge for people who like to visit the gym or a young kid or old-timer who wants to show off. If people see labor as an opportunity to exercise, contribute to the group, and accomplish something, the task will be more enjoyable.

Auto Free Zone Priorities

An AFZ aims to prioritize walking, bicycling, and transit infrastructure. Motorized vehicle lanes within an AFZ can restrict pedestrian access to minimize the chances of an accident between service vehicles, pedestrians, and bicycles. With a low-speed limit, these service vehicle traffic lanes could be located at the edge, under, or over an AFZ to reduce potential conflicts between vehicles, people, and animals.

Auto Free Cargo

Since people won't use cars to move heavy objects within an Auto Free City, other options are required. Electric delivery vehicles, work bikes, rickshaws, bike trailers, and cargo-capable transit are ways to move heavy objects without cars. Within AFZ, people can use electric and person-powered carts to move more oversized items. Auto-free cities could use transport hubs on the edges of Auto Free Cities to organize and prepare parcels for delivery. These transport hubs connect to a transport web nationwide and are integrated into railways, shipyards, and airports. Deliveries can be made to other areas from these hubs on the edge of the city. Cargo-compatible transit could be integrated into auto-free mega-hubs and regions to take advantage of the most efficient ways to people and objects.

Auto Free Examples

Auto-free areas, common over a hundred years ago, are now finding their way into European and South American city centers and selected areas on other continents. Most cities contain parks, universities, and areas around water that don't allow vehicle access. In some towns like Madison, Wisconsin, Berkeley, California, and Brooklyn, New York, auto-free streets contain the most famous street life in the city. Urban planners, visionaries, and forward-looking people are pushing for reductions in the volume and intensity of traffic as people fight to keep their neighborhoods free of the deadly auto plague.

Auto Free Cities

Auto-free cities offer a future where people are more critical than automobiles, and our transport system is safer, more pleasant, and more sustainable. Car-free cities begin with auto-free zones that expand to fill a region. Areas most suited for auto-free activity contain the means to meet needs locally with walkways, bike lanes, and transit that allow people to travel where they want without a car. Global Warming threatens the planet; solutions are needed to address the problem. Auto-free design is an option that replaces pavement with green space, which would reverse the apocalyptic direction we are in now. In terms of transportation, auto-free cities would be safer, healthier, more pleasant, and more efficient than the cities we live in now.

Buying locally

Locating stores, clinics, and services near housing is a way for cities to encourage sustainable transport. If people know where to get what they need locally, they may be more willing to buy locally. These measures can reduce auto use and the cost of transportation. Information that compares driving costs to walking, bicycling, and using transit can influence people's transport choices. If walking to buy food and going to restaurants and clinics is more pleasant, takes less time, and is cheaper than driving, people may be willing to pay a little more to buy locally.

Locating Development

Locating development so that people can meet needs locally is one feature of AFD. Cities that solicit public input about their neighborhood's most relevant shops, restaurants, clinics, and stores are likelier to get what they want. Surveys can be used to draw this information from residents. If people see their input designed into plans, they may be more willing to help implement them. Proactive cities encourage participation from residents and stakeholders.

Criteria for Evaluating a Design

People use criteria to measure, evaluate, and guide development. Some criteria used to assess urban designs include:

- Does it reduce or increase Global Warming?

- How many people, plants, and animals are killed and injured?

- How much pollution enters the air, land, and water?

- What impact does it have on the ecosystem?

- Does it make people, plants, and animals healthier, stronger, and happier?

- Does it make the air, land, and water healthier and stronger?

- Does it move people and goods efficiently with the most minor damage?

- Is it made sustainably using the least environmentally damaging materials and methods?

Over time, some criteria become more relevant than others. Without evaluating the transportation system, we won't know what is wrong and won't know how to fix it. Urban planners use information from stakeholders to guide the designs they create. Criteria can be used to measure whether a transport system is doing what we want and if politicians are doing what we want. This shows what is essential and what makes them distinct from other people.

AUTO FREE CHARRETTE

A charrette is a design process that combines the input of stakeholders to resolve conflicts and make solutions. Design parameters are set in advance. One assumption is that reducing fossil fuel use is a priority for designing, installing, and operating transport infrastructure. An Auto Free Design charrette integrates sustainable transport and development principles into the planning process. A design charrette can begin by identifying problems in the transport system and ways to solve those problems within the constraints of the people who use the system.

Input from the public and stakeholders can influence design and generate support. Urban planners integrate input into the design process. One solution is to reduce auto use in congested areas. Planners could address this by suggesting several solutions:

- Charging money to use congested highways.

- Increase the cost of owning and using a car.

- Improve and expand sustainable transport infrastructure.

A solution is presented to the stakeholders for approval. Eventually, designers develop plans integrating input from the public, stakeholders, and government officials. After final approval, the design is implemented.

Media Conditions People Into Thinking Vehicles are Safe and Without Significant Environmental Impacts

Media forces influence how we move. Most Americans have seen thousands of car commercials before age 10. Movies glorify the pleasures of using a vehicle. Rarely do people see what a hassle it is to break down or get stopped by the police. Some will get a driver's license but have yet to learn how much it costs to own a vehicle or what can happen to them if they don't follow the rules. Governments have much to gain by educating people about the benefits of sustainable transport. Guess how many ads people see promoting walking, bicycling, and using transit? Probably, they see none or few.

Market Forces

Market forces influence the built environment's economic, political, and social conditions. These forces exert a powerful influence on how people use automobiles, transit, and non-motorized transportation. If gas prices rise high enough over a short period, people may reduce or stop auto use and move to other modes. If prices go down, more people may use gas-powered vehicles. Forward-looking governments increase the cost of driving and use the money to prepare for Global Warming, reduce fossil fuel use, and expand sustainable transport and auto-free areas.

Green Cities Minimize Water Pollution from Pavement

Auto Free Cities use an integrated, holistic approach to achieve goals. Water regulation is one example. Now, most buildings drain rainwater into the city storm sewers. Water flows from roofs, sidewalks, and streets into the sewers, then to lakes, rivers, ponds, and water in the area. Toxic materials on roofs and roads concentrate and pollute the ecosystem. So, what does this have to do with transportation? Porous surfaces let water through and can be used instead of pavement. As more water flows through surfaces instead of storm sewers, the water is purified, and less pollution flows into the ecosystem. Water flowing down has less chance to erode the landscape. This increases the health and quality of the air, land, water, plants, and animals.

Auto-Free Cities Reduce The Carbon Footprint of Pavement

Materials for pavement, asphalt, and cement are fossil fuel intensive. Making pavement requires large amounts of fossil fuels. Green cities work to minimize resource use. Most asphalt and concrete are recycled, saving a lot of energy. The goal is to efficiently move people and goods without polluting the ecosystem. One solution is to use fly ash, which has a lower carbon footprint than cement. More frequent maintenance of streets can increase the life of pavement. Looking at the whole lifecycle of the pavement can reveal opportunities for improvement.

Auto Free Cities Increase Habitat for Plants and Animals

Cities with fewer automobiles gain many advantages. As pavement is reduced, more land is available for non-transport functions. Land may be used for urban farms, parks, playgrounds, collectives, and businesses that help people meet needs within walking distance. With less payment, more land is available for green functions.

Auto-free cities give hope to everyone who wants a future for themselves and future generations. People who prefer not to own or use a vehicle will gain. Areas without pavement can reduce work and expense for the city. As people live in areas with fewer cars, the ecosystem gets better as more land is available for non-transport functions.

Chapter 9
Benefits of AFD

To make our planet more sustainable, we can change our transportation system from one dependent on automobiles to one prioritizing walking, bicycling, and using transit. As auto use is reduced and people begin to use more sustainable modes of transport, we will gain many benefits. If we combine a rapid transit system with transit-oriented design, we can create a way for people to walk, bicycle, or use transit to meet their needs.

Regional Impact of Auto-Free Design

To make a safer, healthier, and sustainable city/region, we can change our transportation system from one that depends on automobiles to one that prioritizes non-motorized transport (walking, bicycling) and transit (buses, rail). Reducing auto use while increasing walking, bicycling, and using transit will encourage people to exercise more, reduce pollution, reduce the cost of living, and reduce dependence on scarce resources while improving the quality of the air, land, water, plants, animals, and people.

High Cost of Free Parking Injury, Death and Global Warming

People who walk, ride bicycles, and use transit pay taxes, which pay for parking. Since they don't use that parking, they may be subsidizing car use. When people walk or bicycle, they breathe poisonous vehicle exhaust, which shortens their life span. Vehicles kill and injure many people who walk and bicycle. Car users pay for parking when they pay the parking meter, pay taxes, and for auto use, but the people who walk, bike, and use transit pay a higher price for a system they don't use.

Low and High Density

Sprawl, or low-density development, requires large amounts of infrastructure per capita. Infrastructure includes roads, utilities, and buildings for public services. Public services include the police and fire departments, schools, libraries, and utilities like water and sewer infrastructure. Often, sprawl needs public services that people take for granted in the city. Some city services are stretched beyond capacity as they extend from the city to the suburbs. The more spread out development is, the longer people wait for emergency services that may get stuck in a traffic delay. This lag time caused by traffic congestion can worsen injuries, and some people may die as ambulances and fire trucks are stuck in traffic. Transit-oriented development allows more people to use the transport infrastructure, utilities, and public services. The system may become more efficient as more people use the same infrastructure.

Sprawl May Exclude People Who Can't Afford a Vehicle

When the city spends money to provide infrastructure for low-density development around freeway exits, resources are drained from infrastructure projects within the city. Schools, roads, libraries, and police and fire departments may lose money when the city spends on roads, sewers, and water lines for sprawling developments around freeway exits. As land outside the city is developed, farmland, green space, and rural countryside disappear as highway projects expand auto-oriented development. This destroys the habitat of the earth and water and plants, animals, and people. The soil can't get water, air, or plant life when buried below asphalt and concrete. Suburbs may exclude people because they don't own a vehicle. In some cities, sprawl serves white populations as it drains money for infrastructure projects for minorities in the city.

Sprawl and Sustainable Transport

Sprawl and transit-oriented development are opposites. Sprawl is compatible with an auto-oriented transportation system, while transit-oriented development is compatible with non-motorized transport (walking, bicycling) and transit infrastructure (bus, rail). Sprawl is a low-density development, and transit-oriented design is a high-density development. Living in the suburbs requires auto use, while transit-oriented design does not require auto use.

Auto-free design creates the means for people to live without a car. Fortunately for some, this is the case in many places, but many people still must use a car to live. As regions shift from auto use to non-motorized transport and transit, more people can live without automobiles. As cities increase infrastructure for walking, bicycling, and rapid transit, the benefits will accrue to many people, plants, animals, and the environment.

Infrastructure Liberates Transport from Fossil Fuel Malaise

Fewer cars and less traffic can make our cities safer. If people switch from car use to walking, bicycling, and transit, more people will use safer travel methods. If those people are walking and bicycling in areas that exclude automobiles, they will have less chance of an auto accident. As the region's infrastructure begins to accommodate pedestrians and bicycle users, the region will reduce transportation costs. With fewer roadways to construct, maintain, and patrol, government outlays for transportation will be reduced.

Liberation from the Fossil Fuel Death Machine

Reducing air pollution from vehicles can make regions healthier places to live. Cleaner air can reduce health care costs, pain, suffering, and death for people with respiratory problems and provide better air for plants, animals, and people. Soot from diesel engines damages lungs, plants, and animals while deteriorating the exterior of buildings. Cities can reduce diesel soot pollution by pressuring the Federal government to require diesel engines to use clean technology. Particulate traps and fuel oxidizing technologies reduce diesel soot. Governments that regulate emissions can reduce pain and suffering in people, reduce health care costs, and improve the health of plants, animals, people, and buildings.

Criteria to evaluate our transport system

- How many people, plants, and animals does it kill and injure?

- Does it move people and goods efficiently without pollution?

- How much does it undermine the viability of our environment?

- Can everyone use it?

- Can we move people and objects safely, efficiently, and pleasantly?

- Is it sustainable? Does it sustain the air, land, water, plants, animals, and people? Sustainability is about maintaining and improving the quality of the environment to use it indefinitely.

Priorities of a transport system

- Move people and goods safely without generating pollution.

- Move people and goods using sustainable infrastructure.

- Move people and goods using sustainable methods.

If these changes occur region-wide, significant reductions in healthcare expenditures may accrue. If people walk and bicycle more, healthcare savings will increase as people become healthier by exercising more. Reducing health care costs is a priority for a transport system.

Separation of Motorized and Non-Motorized Transport

Governments can move to separate motorized and non-motorized transport. Many streets pressure pedestrians and bike riders to interact with cars, buses, and trucks. The more we minimize interactions between pedestrians and vehicles or bicycles and vehicles, the safer we will be. Walkways over or under busy streets reduce the chances of an accident between cars and non-motorized transport. Expanding car-free areas will separate automobiles from places where people live and work.

Denial Doesn't Make Problems Disappear

If we begin to admit that the transportation system is causing problems, we can start to resolve those problems. If we don't admit a problem, there will be no reason to make changes. Making changes will result in several benefits. We need to recognize the issues and make changes to receive the benefits.

The Challenge of Living Without a Vehicle

Not everything improves with auto-free design. Some people will lose, and some will gain. People who insist on using automobiles when they can walk, ride bicycles, or use transit may prefer something other than an auto-free system. It may take time for people to adapt. As the economy changes, new jobs will open up for people who lose their careers in the auto industry. An auto-free transport system will generate jobs. Workers will be needed to change the infrastructure, construct and maintain other land uses, and run an expanded transit system.

Towards a Sustainable System

To reduce health care costs, increase the quality of life, and make the city more pleasant, city regions can reduce auto use while increasing non-motorized transport. As the system locates development, which meets needs within walking distance near transit stops, the city region will move closer to a sustainable system.

Infrastructure for Vehicles is Energy Intensive

Walking, cycling, and using transit are more sustainable than auto use. Manufacturing, distributing, and disposing of automobiles require large amounts of resources, energy, and people power. Without a costly, comprehensive, and environmentally damaging system of roads, automobiles will go nowhere. Compare this to another system. Imagine living in an area the size of several blocks with a few streets for service and emergency vehicles but not cars. Parking would be outside an auto-free zone, underground, or in vertical parking lots, and sometimes not at all. Pavement for parking in a car-free area would not be needed, police patrols for auto users would not be needed, less infrastructure would be needed, less health care would be required for the victims of an auto accident, and less industrial production would be generated. As a society, we could live better with less money, less work, and less danger from Global Warming.

Transition to Sustainable

Energy Systems in Sustainable Transport

Fossil fuel use increases the frequency and intensity of storms. Another solution is to move people with electric power from non-fossil fuel sources. Wind and solar farms with batteries could replace the gasoline system. Other non-fossil fuel sources of power could supply energy for transportation. Solar and wind farms could be located near transport refueling stations. Instead of using fossil fuels, clean fuels would be used. This would cut down fossil fuel emissions.

Transition to Sustainable Transport

Corporations May Accelerate the Transition to Self-Driving Electric Vehicles.

Electric self-driving cars may be a huge growth industry for corporations. If this is done on a mass scale, the cost per unit would bring down the price and accelerate the transition to sustainable transport. The government could subsidize the vehicles and increase the pace of the transition. While self driving cars have advantages over person driven cars, auto use provides less advantages then walking and bicycling and using transit. People powered transport is typically better than any other method in terms of the environment and sustainability.

Transition to Sustainable On-Line Electric Vehicles (OLEV)

Tesla tried to do it and didn't quite make it like this. How do you charge a battery without using wires while a vehicle is running? Induction charging plates are mounted on a bus and the road with a 6.7-inch gap between them. This makes a magnetic field that can charge batteries on a bus. You can charge the batteries on the bus while the bus is moving. Since the batteries are constantly changing, you need smaller batteries and may not need to stop so frequently to charge them. Italy and South Korea use this technology to make sustainable transport solutions.

Sustainable Cities Limit Consumption

A sustainable city requires limiting our use of resources so that the environment will support future life. Right now, countries are fighting to control oil, which is a crucial element in the auto economy, but reduces the viability of the environment. The quest for oil undermines a just, equitable, and democratic foreign policy. As oil resources dwindle, the fight to control oil will intensify, but this drive to control the resource could be reduced if we pursue other ways of moving people and goods. An auto-free economy reduces oil use, conserves energy, and uses renewable energy sources.

Sustainable Transport Improves the Standard of Living

In the dominant economy, many work more for less money and pay more for everything. Paying for a vehicle can break the budget and make life unaffordable as people struggle to pay rent, transport, insurance, utilities, food, clothing, and health care. When people can walk, bicycle, or use transit to move themselves and goods, they may have more money to pay the bills. This can raise the standard of living.

Sustainable Transport Can Make Cities Competitive

Cities compete with other cities worldwide for jobs, resources, and funding. When cities reduce the cost of transport, the cost of living may decrease. People will have more money to spend on other things, and cities may gain a competitive edge over cities with higher living costs. If workers need less money for transportation, they will be able to afford other things. Workers with less transport costs may not need the wages of a worker who must use an automobile.

Sustainable Transport and Competitive Cities

Reducing health care and transportation costs can be done in many regions with effort. If the city sets up the conditions for people to walk, bicycle, and use transit to meet their needs, they will get more exercise, and this can reduce visits to clinics and hospitals. Cities can be set up so people can meet their needs a short distance away. As businesses struggle to compete with workers from other countries who live on a lot less money, companies can make lower wages go further by helping workers meet their needs. Pressuring the city to provide sustainable transportation is in the interest of the companies that compete with other regions worldwide. Regions that reduce transport and healthcare costs will have a competitive edge over auto-oriented areas.

Goals of Auto-Free Design

Auto-free design moves from a transport system where people must use an automobile to live to a transportation system that allows people to live without a car. A better transportation system is one in which non-motorized transport and transit are the fastest, cheapest, and most sustainable way to move between destinations. In cities and rural areas worldwide, people must own a vehicle to work, go to school, shop, and go to clinics. One way to increase freedom is to create the means for people to live without owning an automobile.

Auto Free Design Goals Examples

- Reduce pavement by 1% per year

- Increase Walk Infrastructure 2-10% per year

- Increase Bicycle Infrastructure 2-10% per year

- Increase Transit Infrastructure 2-10% per year

- Increase Green Space by 1% per year

- Reduce Fossil Fuel Use in Vehicles 1% per year then...

- Reduce miles traveled with vehicles 1%, 5% per year then...

- Increase walkways to transit 1-5% per year

- Increase bike lanes by 5% or 10 miles per year

- Increase bike parking near transit 1-5% per year

- Increase trips made by walking 1-3% per year

- Increase trips done with bicycles 1-10% per year

- Increase trips made with transit 1-10% per year

- Reduce parking lanes 1% per year

Did Someone Mention Efficiency

Consider this;

- A bicycle weighs 30 lbs and can move 300 lb. or ten times its weight.

- A car weighs 3000 lbs and can move 850 lbs or less than 1/3 of its weight.

A bicycle uses human power, and a car uses fossil fuel power. A car may be powered by green power, and some are self-drive. An E-bike is an electric power bicycle. The person-powered bicycle may be the most efficient, especially if you consider health improvements from riding a bicycle.

High Cost of Free Parking; Injury, Death, and Global Warming

People who walk, ride bicycles, and use transit pay taxes, which pay for parking. Since they don't use that parking, they are subsidizing car use. When people walk or bicycle, they breathe poisonous vehicle exhaust, which shortens their life span. Vehicles kill and injure many people who walk and bike. Car users pay for parking when they pay the parking meter, pay taxes, and for auto use, but the people who walk, bicycle, and use transit pay a high price for a system they don't use.

Texting While Walking Generates Safety Problems

As people walk while texting, attention to safety diminishes. In New York City, it's common to see people walking in the street with their eyes on screens instead of how to avoid collisions with pedestrians, bike riders, skateboarders, vendors wheeling huge carts, cars, trucks, buses, dogs, and motorcycles. In the chaos of traffic, full attention is needed to make transport safe.

Talking on the Phone While Driving a Car Generates Safety Problems

Talking on the phone takes attention from driving. Without using a phone, drivers make mistakes that kill 40,000 people and injure 3 Million. Imagine what happens when another distraction is added. Enforcing the law may be quite challenging, but call logs may leave an indelible trace. In the quest to sell more vehicles to make more money, car producers add more gadgets that reduce attention to driving.

Benefits of Auto-Free Design

For people to live without an automobile, shops, restaurants, and clinics can be located within walking distance of housing and transit. If many people live in a small area, there will be enough people to keep shops and clinics open. To do this requires high densities of people and mixed-use development. Mixed-use development allows different kinds of land uses to occupy the same area. People can live next to the grocery store, restaurant, clothing store, or clinic. Many cities still need to allow this and were set up when mixed-use zoning wasn't familiar or desirable. In those cities, single-use zoning is more common. Single-use zoning does not allow residential housing to mix with office space, restaurants, or clinics. In these areas, the distances between shops and housing are so large that people must use a car.

In Sprawling Developments, Walking, Bicycling, and Using Transit May be Impossible or Impractical

Auto-free design combines sustainable transport with sustainable development. Walking and bicycling are sustainable transportation. Transit use is more sustainable than auto use. Transit-oriented development is more sustainable than sprawl. Auto-free development, which allows people to meet their needs without a car, is more sustainable than transit-oriented development. One can think about sustainability in terms of the choices people have that they didn't have before. Often, sprawling developments do not allow people to walk, bicycle, or use transit to travel. By choosing not to use fossil fuels, we can avoid the problems of Global Warming.

Advantages of Walking, Bicycling, and Using Transit

Auto-free design is a progressive direction for transportation and development that offers several advantages and can lead to a brighter future. Sustainable transport, which includes walking, cycling, and using transit, is safer, healthier, and more sustainable than car use. Sustainable transportation can lead to a more stable, secure, and viable environment, economic system, and foreign policy. Auto use is killing and injuring many people and pushing us into difficult and dangerous environmental, economic, and foreign policy circumstances. We can begin a path to a brighter future by making relatively minor changes now.

3 Actions Toward a Brighter Future

- Reduce Auto Use

- Increase Walk, Bicycle and Transit Infrastructure

- Transit Oriented Development

What changes move us to an auto-free city? Three currents of action will move us toward a better future. Reducing auto use, increasing sustainable transport, and transit-oriented development will make a safer, cleaner, and more efficient way to make people and goods. Governments that care about the future should take measures to reduce auto use. Increasing the costs of using an automobile by changing the tax code, charging tolls in congested areas, and improving sustainable transport infrastructure are ways to reduce auto use. Providing better walkways and bike lanes integrated into a regional rapid transit system can create the conditions for people to live without automobiles. As appropriate development is situated around transit stops, people can meet their needs without leaving their neighborhood.

Moving Toward Sustainable Development

Auto-free design moves from an auto-oriented transportation and development system to one that allows people to walk to meet their needs. It avoids coercive measures and favors participation. If transit infrastructure is set up to enable people to travel cheaper, faster, and more efficiently by walking, bicycling, and using transit, even car users will choose transit. Cities that want to create a brighter future for their citizens can integrate auto-free design into their long-term plans. The cities, corporations, and nonprofit organizations that are the first to incorporate these designs will have an edge over other cities as auto-free cities reduce transport and healthcare expenses per capita. The first ones to develop the auto-free direction can export those ideas and actions to other locations.

Transition to Auto Free

A gradual process can transform a region from auto-need to auto-free. The main flows of transport, trade, and development come from a consensus that integrates the short and long-term interests of the stakeholders in the region. Reducing pavement by 1% per year is one option. Unused parking lots and parking lanes can be converted to other land uses. Changes can emerge from the top down and the bottom up as people define the means and ends that fit the neighborhood. The city can offer suggestions, designs, tax breaks, and other incentives for people to walk, bicycle, and use transit.

Combining Sustainable Transport and Development

Auto-free design is impossible without thoughtful, relevant, and appropriate development. Other cities with more advanced sustainable transport infrastructure could provide inspiration and guidance. While high-density development is a way to think about auto-free infrastructure, lower densities are also possible. Stakeholders and designers should make the plan. Sustainable development, which balances economic goals with long-term environmental viability, must be a part of this equation. Until transportation and development resonate sustainably, regions will be headed toward the Global Warming apocalypse.

Sustainable Transport Competitions and Civic Pride

To bolster support for bike lanes and walkways, cities in the Netherlands sponsor competitions to encourage and excite participation to expand support for walkways and bike lanes and transit infrastructure. Competitors and supporters demonstrate support for bike lanes and walking and transit infrastructure. Media generated by the event builds support for sustainable transport, which may come under attack from the auto industry and people who don't like bicycles. Educating the public about walking and riding safely, distributing maps, and providing training on bicycle safety are done at these events. Forward-leaning government galvanizes public support with intercity sustainable transport competitions.

Generating Public Support

A challenge is integrating the auto industry and car users to adopt sustainable modes of transport. For auto-free design to work, people must be a part of the process. The public, private, and nonprofit sectors can create the means to transfer people from the auto industry to the auto-free world. That connection is the means to make sustainable transportation happen. Ideally, the automakers would seize the opportunity to develop sustainable transport infrastructure. Transit, buses, rail cars, and person-powered vehicles are needed to move the next generations of citizens. Roads, parking lots, and pavement can be converted to relevant and appropriate land uses as defined by the stakeholders in the area. The more people embrace practical, relevant, appropriate, and necessary action, the more everyone will gain.

Of course, little, if anything, will happen without a concerted effort from politicians, media, corporations, nonprofits, religious groups, and the public. Making all this real may be a long shot, or an inevitable consequence of regressive thought and action as weather patterns, Global Warming, and climate change begin to dictate what happens.

Sustainable Infrastructure

Within the context of our society, few things are sustainable. Plants, animals, and people may sustain themselves, but most production is done with unsustainable methods. Steel, concrete, and electronics production requires large amounts of fossil fuels. That fossil fuel use is rapidly destroying our ability to live. Sustainable infrastructure may be built with sustainable methods. This challenge can be won if people work together to make it happen.

Power for Sustainability: America's Rural Electric Coops

Rural Electric Coops, which began under Franklin Delano Roosevelt in the 1940s, integrated clean power into the grid. Solar and wind farms charge batteries for electric vehicle fueling stations. As Cooperatives seek a local, green source of energy instead of fossil fuels, many won't have to breathe fossil fuel pollution and support the corrupt oil machine. Electric co-ops are member-owned and produce high-value solutions for their members.

Chapter 10
AFD How to Get Rid of Your Car

Cars can be useful, but at a certain point, they become useless for the safety, budget, and power of people to transport. Most urban areas of the country were designed for vehicle traffic, with little consideration for people who walk, bicycle, and use transit. Other areas in small towns or well-designed urban areas make it easy for people to live without a vehicle. Transitioning from auto use to auto-free living can be challenging for people who have never considered it. For others, it's a minor adjustment if they live in an area that prioritizes infrastructure for people who walk, bicycle, or use transit. So how can I get rid of my car?

How to Get Rid of Your Car

- Walk, bicycle, and use transit to meet needs and wants.

- Move to an area with good walking, bicycling, and transit infrastructure.

- Make a list of trips you make with a vehicle and begin making those trips by walking, bicycling, or using transit.

- Make a list of car trips, cross out the ones you don't need or want, and do the rest by walking, bicycling, and using transit.

- Stop using your car and see what happens; give the keys to someone else and see how long you can go without using a vehicle.

- Set goals to reduce auto use, keep a log to govern your progress, and track vehicle costs.

Learn to Use and Enjoy the Benefits of Walking

If you are used to driving a car, walking may seem like a Neanderthal way of moving. Starting small may yield results. Make a list of places to walk. The list may include going to work, visiting a friend, or finding a spot less traveled. Take what you need to transport what you are getting. If you are moving a refrigerator, take a refrigerator dolly; if you are carrying food, a backpack or hand cart could work. If the trip seems like too much, do a practice walk so you know where to go without using a map. Enjoy the benefits of fresh air, and enjoy time to look at the flora, fauna, buildings, and ecosystem. Feel the pleasure of being outside and experiencing people as they meander through the day, hear the call of the wild, and see what is left to be done. Find what animals and plants can withstand the human onslaught. Still, you might wonder, "Is it worth it, or what's the point?"

Walking is the most sustainable way of transport. It requires the least infrastructure, least investment, and generates the highest return. A sidewalk requires less materials, energy, and money than a roadway for cars. Also, walking on shredded wood, crushed rock, or an informal path is possible. Non-paved walkways made with shredded wood and crushed rock put less strain on your body. This can reduce healthcare costs and allow people to exercise more. You gain the most because you don't need to buy anything; you energize your body with exercise and learn about your neighborhood as you walk. As you feel the benefits of walking, you may realize how you can end the burden of car use while exercising more and becoming intimate with your immediate surroundings.

Learn to Use and Enjoy the Benefits of Bicycling

For many, riding a bicycle is freedom, especially if you have the skill and can ride with just enough fear to keep safe. Riding a bike is not for everyone, but has many advantages for those who dare. In some urban areas with slow traffic, riding a bicycle is the fastest way to get between destinations. With caution, safety gear, and some planning, you can minimize danger. Some people ride for many years without a serious accident. A lot depends on the infrastructure. With protected bike lanes and controlled traffic, getting exercise, feeling the outdoors, and reaching your destination faster than walking, driving a car, or using transit is possible. Bicycling can feel empowering when you cruise by vehicles stuck in traffic. One way to increase your safety is to chant in your mind, "SAFETY, SAFETY, SAFETY," anytime your mind begins to wonder. If you increase the distance between you and pedestrians, bicycles, and vehicles, you may reduce your chances of an accident. Stay out of the way of everyone else. Make way for pedestrians. When you are close to a pedestrian, try slowing down to their speed. Keep alert in areas with little traffic; you never know when a pothole, speeding driver, or animal crossing the road will pop up. If you can run machines well, you could make a good biker, or if you like sports and have enough awareness and caution to drive safely. Some people ride in the rain and snow. If this is done at night, the danger increases more. While I've done it for many years without injuries, it's hazardous, but it can be done safely. Another option for many is to use bicycles with other modes of transport.

Bicycling integrates well with walking, transit, and auto use. Walk and bicycle to exercise different muscles, get a biker's eye for the area, and take advantage of both modes of transport. Many buses, subways, and trains allow bikes. You can bicycle to transit and bicycle from transit to your destination. In this case, you exercise, take a break in transit, and get more exercise. It's a triple win, but can it be used for more than recreation?

Bicycles are practical work vehicles that allow you to haul significant loads with the least energy. Mount a basket on the front or back, carry a backpack, or hook up a trailer to increase your load. Bicycles are great for running errands because you can easily find a parking space, load up quickly, and go. It's the easiest way to get a lot of work done efficiently: to move your body and stuff from point A to point b in the least time with the least effort and the most minor environmental consequence. Overall, bicycle transport provides a significant and effective way to reduce or eliminate auto use.

Muscular Bodies Resist Hazards of Bike Riding

Pollution is debilitating in traffic in dense urban areas, especially in the summer. Construction dust, dirt, vehicle exhaust, garbage truck vomit, and smelly garbage and debris on the bike path can make it difficult to concentrate on traffic. Potholes can throw you off the bike, especially if it's cold and wet with ice. Traveling in the rain and snow and at night is also challenging. If you enjoy or do well with danger, a bicycle could benefit you. It's good to stay in shape so if you hit the pavement; you can get up and walk away. Building up your core, legs, and shoulders is worth the effort. Still, if you ride by the rules, you may ride for many years without a problem, but if you tend to be more like a stuntperson, you should ride with the brakes on.

Auto Free Design

Learn to Use and Enjoy the Benefits of Transit

For those who have yet to use transit, it may seem like a bother when you are used to getting into your car and zooming off; however, under the right conditions, using transit is safer, less stressful, cheaper, and more accessible than driving a car. Think about it; on the commuter bus, you can eat, sleep, read, or let your mind wander as you look out the window. You don't have to worry about your vehicle breaking down, someone crashing into you, or when you will have to shell out big bucks for a repair, car insurance, traffic violation, or an accident. You have less stress, and that makes the ride more pleasant. Professional drivers drive buses. Many go the same route every day and know how to avoid accidents and reach their destination safely. Because you are in a massive vehicle, if you are in an accident, you have less chance of being injured or killed. Walking and bicycling integrate well with transit.

List the time, money, and resources required to use your vehicle.

According to the American Automobile Association, driving a car costs about $.5, 50 cents per mile, including the vehicle's cost, insurance, gas, oil, and maintenance. Other costs people may need to consider are:

- The stress of driving.
- The impact of pollution.
- The time it takes to find parking.
- The time to get the car fixed.
- The danger of using the car around the house.

By making a list of time, energy, materials, effort, and expense to own, maintain, operate, and finally dispose of the vehicle and toxic waste, you can better understand the actual cost of owning and using a car. This can lead to an honest and beneficial examination of whether or not a car is worth having.

How much time does it take to buy and use a vehicle

- time to research to find the right car
- time to research to find the best deal
- time to research insurance company and insurance to pay insurance when due
- time to buy the car and register it properly
- time to deal with tickets, increase insurance costs
- time to healing from injury, burying a friend, relative
- time to make money to pay for tickets, accidents, mechanics, lawyers, doctors, insurance, car dealers....
- time to find or buy parking
- time to find a mechanic to maintain the car
- time to bring the car to a mechanic to maintain it
- time to pay traffic tickets, including going to court
- time to get car insurer to pay up after an accident
- time to watch car commercials

I do things while I wait for the bus

- fix my bike,

Auto Free Design

- do exercises
- talk to people
- eat food
- meditate
- make phone calls
- take notes
- relax and recover from capitalism
- be happy I'm not wasting time on a car

Cost of buying a car

- payment for the car, taxes, insurance, and registration
- cost of finance charges and dealership fees
- if it's a new car, car depreciates 10-30% after you drive it around the block

Cost of Maintaining and Using a Car

- payments for gas, oil, brake fluids, and other costs
- money for car insurance
- pay for vehicle safety and emissions checks.
- cost of parking and driving tickets.
- pay for medical bills for accidents.
- pay for lawyer bills for contesting tickets and accidents
- pay for funeral and related expenses when someone dies

Make a list of reasons why you don't like to drive.

I read a statistic that said if you drive a car once every 14 years, you will be in a car crash. Most people know more than a few people who've been killed or injured in a car crash. Others know what a hassle it is when it breaks down in the middle of nowhere, and you are at the mercy of who you can find to help you, especially in the winter when it's below freezing. Some people get annoyed when they have to find and use an auto repair shop to fix their car. Now, what about that significant upfront investment? How many people can shell out $1-50,000 for a car? This is for an investment that only loses value over time, especially if it's brand new.

Why Get Rid of Your Car (Make Your List)

- To increase your safety

- To increase your time

- To get more exercise

- To get more money

- To have more fun

- To have less stress

How to Get Rid of Your Car

Some use a sledgehammer, others dynamite, some just run it off a cliff, and wise ones take it to the junkyard. Selling is an option if you want to continue the use of a deadly, eco-suicide machine. Finally, with electricity, we can rid ourselves of the fossil fuel cancer destroying the country, but even electric cars are mostly unsustainable. Yes, cars generate many advantages, but overall, including electricity, a brighter future excludes vehicles from the built environment and takes advantage of more straightforward, healthier, cleaner ways of transport.

How to Get Rid of Your Car (make your list)

- Sell it on Craigslist.
- Donate it to Kars4Kids or some other non-profit.
- Walk, bicycle, and use transit until it has no use.
- Move to a transit-friendly area and stop using a vehicle.
- Shop, work, and live locally.
- Use help from family, friends, and coworkers.
- Organize your trips and make a goal and plan.

Make an Auto Free Log

Writing down your goals and taking steps to realize them can help you stay motivated, observe results, and keep you on target. A log enables you to learn where you are coming from and going. Each day, make a list of what you want to accomplish. Keep it short, simple, and doable. If it's a big task, break it down and give yourself time to make it happen. Approach it like you will enjoy doing it. If you keep a list of mistakes, you won't repeat them. You can share the log with other like-minded people so they realize it might not be as difficult as it seems. Taking photos and videos can make it more memorable. You can celebrate the day you get rid of the car and each year on the anniversary. Keep detailed notes about struggles, triumphs, and sentiments. As you progress, you will gain motivation as you become aware of your successes. One day, you can refer back to it and realize the benefits of becoming auto-free.

Trip List

Getting organized can make the process easier. Make a list of trips you make. This list may include going to work, schools, restaurants, and clinics. If possible, plot them on a map. From this list, make a list of the trips you could walk, bicycle, or ride transit. Rank each trip according to the level of difficulty in making the trip without a car. Include a number from 1-10, 10 being the most difficult. Start accomplishing the easier ones to gain momentum. Use creativity to move through problems. As you compare the costs of using alternatives to car use, keep in mind all the related costs of using a car. Doing this may make you realize the advantages of not using a vehicle.

Make a plan and do it.

Another simple answer is this: Make a plan and do it. I want to reduce my car use by 50% in 2 years, 2 months, or 20 minutes. A plan needs a goal and a period to realize that goal. I plan to use transit, bicycle, or walk to get what I need and want within two months. Then, I will list smaller goals to reach the larger goal.

Getting Motivated

If there's a will, there's a way. For people who have struggled for years to buy, operate, and maintain a vehicle, motivation to avoid dealing with car problems may be strong, but only if they know it's possible to get out of their situation. With a viable plan in mind, fueled with a desire for a more pleasant, less stressful, and more environmentally friendly way to move around, one can make it easier to reach the goal.

Carry out Your Plan.

Keep your plan in mind

- memorize it
- meditate on it in the morning and night

- talk about it

- write it down

- map it out

- keep at it day and night

Once you have a plan and a goal in mind and your motivation revved up, it's time to move into action. Remember, this project may take years, and what's important is to take little steps to move to the goal. You can't give up; you must keep going, even after it feels like you are going backward. Sometimes, you have to make a bunch of mistakes to continue forward. You may have to start over three times, but that doesn't matter; it just means you will learn more. Keep looking at why you get lost, confused, and downtrodden. Look at the goal every day and night. Concentrate on it, look at your plan, and make revisions as you do research, learn from others, and chart a path to live auto-free. It's likely that you will have more time, energy, and money after you get rid of your vehicle. Living with less stress is a huge benefit. Meditating on the goal will generate creative ways to get through problems. Part of the process is to imagine something else. Talking about it helps realize the goal. If people hear that you are motivated and excited and have a reason to live, they will be excited and help you achieve your goal.

People Power is the most Sustainable.

Walking is the most sustainable transport since it requires the least infrastructure and provides the most benefits. Vehicle pavement requires vast amounts of fossil fuels, raw materials, and public resources. A sidewalk requires much less because it is smaller and has a smaller load to carry. Vehicles also impact humans. Auto use requires less physical activity. According to Wikipedia, almost 40% of the US is obese. Car driving makes obesity worse. Walking, running, bicycling, and using transit requires more personpower than driving a vehicle. Using energy to move your body is good exercise, which generates many health benefits. Exerting force can make you feel empowered and more confident as you go beyond to achieve something you've never done before. Walking integrates people into the neighborhood as they meet their neighbors, play with pets, and discuss the issues of the day. Using a car generates more health problems than walking, bicycling, and using transit. Prevention is the best healthcare. Exercise can help prevent heart disease, cancer, diabetes, and obesity and give you the energy to do other things. As people reduce the miles they drive, the benefits accrue. The quality of life improves with less stress and more time to enjoy the life around us.

Getting rid of your car can reduce stress while increasing your time and money. Many urban areas provide infrastructure to live without a car, but some need to. Living in these areas usually means you depend on people with vehicles, which can work if you are flexible. Better governance in areas without transit can make it possible to live without a car. As more people live without vehicles, the environment may improve.

People seek to meet needs sustainably in the community and want their children to grow up in a viable environment. As of July 2020, ignorance, denial, and corruption are speeding the country to climate change catastrophes. People of sound mind are moving to live sustainably and refuse to follow backward leaders.

About the Author

Author information:

Dan Paul explores progressive, radical and sustainable solutions to the dominant paradigm. After 20 years of living and working in cooperative communities in Madison, San Francisco and NYC, he wrote this book to advance green solutions. With  a degree in Sustainable Transport and Development and years of experience cofounding Dreamtime Village, Bolozone and Urbana Indymedia center, he has combined practical experience and book learning to make this book come alive. For decades, he has worked on making affordable housing in disadvantaged communities. His work has been published in the Radical History Review, SMILE magazine and Desire Actualized: Foundations of Alternative Action, and the Journal of Pataphysical Succulentosophy.

Also by Dan Paul

Philosophy of Action Design and Multiplicity by Dan Paul

Book 1 Auto Free Design

Book 2 Workers Health Handbook

Book 3 Save Your Life Prevent Hospital Use

Book 4 Coop Owners Handbook

Book 5 Eye on AI Meeting Needs Sustainably

Book 6 Travels on the Nomadic Terrain

Book 7 Tales of the Urban Shaman

Book 8 Housing in the Danger Zone

Book 9 Corona Time

Book 10 Philosophy of Design, Action and Multiplicity

Coming soon

Landlords Against Eviction

Auto Free USA

Websites

https://viaradmedia.org

https://autofreedesign.com

http://workershealthhandbook.com

http://sylphu.com

Social Media

https://www.facebook.com/profile.php?id=61555599616489

https://twitter.com/jonblu

https://www.instagram.com/jonblu61/Book 2

www.ingramcontent.com/pod-product-compliance
Lightning Source LLC
LaVergne TN
LVHW041256080426
835510LV00009B/754